Theology for Skeptics

Theology for Skeptics

Reflections on God

DOROTHEE SOELLE

TRANSLATED BY
JOYCE L. IRWIN

FORTRESS PRESS
Minneapolis

THEOLOGY FOR SKEPTICS
Reflections on God

Biblical translations employed in this translation are given with the
citations, except where adapted by the author.

Cover design: Evans McCormick Creative
Author photograph: Brigitte Friedrich
Cover graphic: Dan Mason, "Forest," 1993, oil on linen

Library of Congress Cataloging-in-Publication Data
Sölle, Dorothee.
[Es muss doch mehr als alles geben. English]
Theology for skeptics : reflections on God / Dorothee Soelle.
p.   cm.
Translation of: Es muss doch mehr als alles geben.
Includes bibliographical references.
ISBN 0–8006–2788–1
1. God. 2. Sölle, Dorothee. I. Title.
BT102.S57313 1994
231–dc20
                                                94–2828
                                                CIP

Manufactured in Great Britain   AF 1–2788
                        4   5   6   7   8   9   10

CONTENTS

CHAPTER 1

Speaking of God

TO SPEAK about God — that is what I would like to do
and where I always fail. That is what I have been
attempting for years, in the language of women, in the
language of the disenfranchised and of the handicapped,
in the language of my tradition that I love, which begins
with Isaiah and does not end with the Middle Ages. Yet
I almost never succeed in this "God-talk."

I want to recount one of my defeats in this matter,
which took place on a day in the late 1980s during a
long taxi ride straight through Berlin. The young taxi
driver appeared surly and was stubbornly silent. When
something came over the radio about a high-ranking
military visitor from NATO finally coming to Berlin, the
driver commented sarcastically that that was exactly
what was needed. I wanted to know whether he now —
after the opening of the Berlin Wall — would have to
go into the military. As if this question had been the
key to his heart, he let loose, saying that no government
would bring him to that point again. He had sat around
for three years in the National People's Army, for
which everything actually always stayed the same
anyway and the people on the top made themselves
rich. "Right now they are raising their per diem allow-
ances again." In every system the poor people are
always the ones who get ripped off — that had become

clear to him. Those on top have only one interest, and that is to remain on top at any cost. "They want to wreck everything". It doesn't matter to them when the whole thing here blows up, the ozone hole; it can't go on this way much longer anyhow. Human beings — "Don't make me laugh!" — are such a design failure; it can't take much longer.

At first I tried to intervene and say there were other human beings who were rising up against injustice and the destruction of the earth, but he wouldn't listen to any of that. I said I had worked for years in the peace movement, but he had no interest in that. I referred to a few young people I know in the east, in the former German Democratic Republic, who preferred to do alternative service rather than to go along with everything that was coming from the top. But he was caught up in a world of hopelessness and didn't want to know anything about the freedom to decide. To go along or to swim against the stream — what did either one accomplish? His private situation — his wife had lost her job, there was no room in any kindergarten for his child, they were being threatened with a rise in rent and eviction from their apartment — was not the only thing that made the world so detestable to him. "My earnings aren't bad," he stated matter-of-factly, but his anger concerning the similarities of systems (the new surprisingly like the old) combined with his apocalyptic view of the destruction of the earth to result in what in the Middle Ages might have been called "hatred of God."

I kept on trying: "Not all people want to continue on as before: I have friends, and we all think much like you do, but we draw other conclusions. We resist this craving for more death." But nothing made any impression on him. My last timid attempt went something like this: "You know, I am a Christian, and I simply don't believe that this is the way it was meant

to be; God, you understand, doesn't want it this way."
He began to laugh; he laughed loudly with a forced
attempt at controlling his laughter. I had to get out, but
I still asked him how he had voted. "For the D-Mark,"
he said bitterly. "And your child?" I asked suddenly, as
if a remnant of God must still be hidden somewhere.
He shrugged his shoulders.

I have asked myself why I was unable to share God
with this person. Why I can't pass on my hope, my
strength, my joy, my "despite-everything." There must
be something wrong; if God is really God, then God is
"that which is most communicable," as Meister Eckhart
said. So I don't need to sit silently in a taxi and be
embarrassed to utter such a big word. Has it become
impossible in our modern age to speak about God? Does
every young person who grew up in the former East
Germany know that talk about God is nonsense? And
is it any different in the western part of Germany? Is
there no comprehensible, communicable language for
the inner mystery of reality? Has it become impossible
to say that something comforts and supports us, that
we are not alone with our desires and our longing for
another life where we don't have to deal with one
another like wolves?

I don't really believe that; I have other experiences
also. I meet people who, through their behavior, their
manner of dealing with creation and with their neigh-
bors, communicate something about God, even if for
understandable reasons they may not use the word *God*.
It is too sullied, misused, bandied about, and printed
on every dollar, which is probably where it belongs.
And yet people share with me the strength of God they
carry within themselves: their warmth, their readiness
to undergo risks, their eyes alert to every flower that
still grows through the asphalt.

About which God are we actually speaking?

Dorothee Soelle

A basic idea of the Reformation tradition is that we are always involved with something resembling God — either with the God of life or with an idol that acts as if it were all-powerful and determined everything. When I think about the conversation with the young taxi driver, I see the idol very clearly before me. It sucks the blood of people. It has made them blind and evil; they greedily make themselves wealthy, they arm themselves pathologically and, deaf to the crying, they let children starve. None of this matters to the idol, who is incomprehensible, unintelligible fate. There is no God, this perspective says. There is no hope; justice and love are sentimental illusions. We live under fate, a destiny that runs its course whether or not we assent to it.

I want to introduce here another experience which likewise has to do with an idol, even though the orientation and setting come out of a completely different worldview. This story takes place among the poor in the glitter of Manhattan; it concerns a visit which I made together with a young pastor to a home in one of the public housing projects which still existed in New York City until the end of the 1970s.

On a visit among the poor
in the glitter of Manhattan

In a new house of the city
built for slum dwellers
we look for Michael
the elevator is out of order again
we climb up eleven stories
the graffiti on the unpainted walls
and aggressive
Michael drinks beer he's a New Yorker
he laughs and was in Viet Nam
how long I ask and know already
too long

he shows us how clean his kitchen is
his wife left three years ago
he is raising three children
he calls them in one at a time
has them stand to attention and asks
who is the boss who
has the say who
commands here do you love me
after four questions they may again
go play.

Do you believe in God I ask him
if I were not so despairing about what I see
I wouldn't have to ask
actually not to speak of he replies
but still there must finally be one
who commands and is the boss mustn't there
there must be one on top he says
would you go back to Viet Nam

I ask for a year and a half he has been
unemployed
I hated it but of course
if necessary I would go back
and your son I want to know
if Uncle Sam needs him then
he will go
and Bruce my pale young Baptist preacher
prays with Michael for him and us all
that he will find work and soon he says
and I pray that he will lose his god
finally and for always.

Who is this god of a dark-skinned man in Manhattan?
Actually Michael doesn't believe in God; he doesn't
want to be identified with churchgoers. But then he
does concoct something, perhaps from his childhood

11

religious memories but more from his own life experience. Someone has to be the boss. Power, authority, command — those are the most important attributes of his God. No sentimentality, no suffering, no passion, not even the slightest remembrance of the child in the manger or the half-starved landless *campesino,* as the crucified Christ is depicted by many Latin Americans. Seldom has anyone spoken to me so clearly, so matter-of-factly, so unceremoniously as this Vietnam veteran of the false God, the "Lord who rules all," the masculine idol. "Someone must be on top," he says, and it hasn't the least bit to do with justice or mercy. It is, in theistic mode (and most Americans believe, as everyone knows, in something they call God), precisely what his younger but just as desperate brother from East Berlin believes without appealing to a higher authority.

Yet there is a difference between the two stories and an indication of how we are to answer the question of *which* God we are actually speaking about. This difference arises through my student and friend who took me with him into the slums. He does not try, as I did in the taxi, to testify about God. He prays with the people whom he visits, and sometimes I think there is no other method. The difference I am referring to consists in changing the original question: posed correctly, it would read, *"To* which God are we really speaking?" We can only speak *about* God when we speak *to* God.

When we had managed the stairs
they stank of urine and garbage
joe limps toward us
an old man twice as thin as I
he had been reading a religious book
but difficult words like colossians and circumcision
he didn't know and he looked them up in his bible
his eyes are weak

as we sit with him a while
I hear that he is only forty-four
but drugs and alcohol have not
left much of him remaining
he chain smokes and whistles through a white tube
that extends out of his throat.

He tells of his great aunt in georgia
he would like to be at her burial there
he speaks of the plants he would like to have
a few for spring and then one
that blooms in summer and then these permanent ones
the apartment is bare two hand towels hang
from the clothesline across the middle of the room the
children
from the building paid him a visit afterward
the radio was gone

In case he drinks again his heart
won't be able to handle it in case the
food stamps for the poor
are done away with in the interest of an ordered
balance sheet
he won't eat anything more.

My student and friend the pale baptist
prays for him and for us
and give joe he says to god what he needs
and above all your kingdom.

To which God are we really speaking? At a conference
there was a group of women conversing about religious
questions. One asked where God had been at Auschwitz. A young woman from the evangelical camp, who
described herself as a believer, answered with the sentence: "Auschwitz was willed by God." Everyone was
appalled and wanted to know how she meant that.
"Quite simply," she said, "if God had not willed it, it

would not have happened. Nothing happens without God." The Wholly Other God has so determined it, and though we cannot understand it we must accept it in humility. God's authority, lordship, and omnipotence may not be placed in doubt, it is not for us to inquire after God's providential will. The God who is completely independent from all God's creatures has willed everything that happens. God and God alone could have hindered it. But God's ways are not our ways.

This manner of speaking about God sounds pious, but it doesn't really get anyone anywhere. It solidifies hierarchical thinking into authorities and power. It makes us into impotent nobodies on whose lives nothing actually depends. In reality *everything* depended on the lives and behavior of people in Germany for the victims of our actions. In reality everything relating to the preservation of this earth depends on the lives and behavior of people in the rich world. We are involved; we are responsible. The belief of the young fundamentalist woman is in fact not very different from the apocalyptic doomsday belief of my taxi driver. In both modes of thinking our role as victims of an inscrutable giant machine is the same. The same thing that triggered frustration and anger in the taxi driver is accepted by her out of devotion to the incomprehensible. Submission without a say in the matter is common to both. Both are fixated on power and cannot think in terms of shared power, which we can also call love. For the young woman God is the sovereign Lord who would have intervened from above, had God so willed. Since God did not intervene, God must have willed Auschwitz. The most important thing about God is God's power.

I am reminded by this way of thinking about God of a cheeky song from Vienna, in which a young man from a wealthy home carries out all possible mischief

at the expense of others and then in the refrain sings
reassuringly: "Papa will set things right." Many
believers have never gone beyond this childish image of
God; they have never learned to assume responsibility
themselves. Their relationship to God remains childish;
they do not want to be friends of God but want to
remain subordinates and dependents.

But must we really speak in this way? God is mighty,
we are helpless — is that all? A few years ago I had a
meeting in a church congregation near Hamburg in
which we recalled *Kristallnacht*, the night when Jewish
homes, businesses, and synagogues were vandalized in
1938, prefiguring and inaugurating the full terror of the
Holocaust. A woman turned up and introduced herself
as an outsider. She told how she had struggled for years
with the Jewish–Christian problem because she wanted
to know how it came to the point of Shoah, the extermi-
nation of European Jews. She ended her contribution
with the words, "When I had understood Auschwitz, I
joined the peace movement." In this statement I found
a different God from the omnipotent Lord of heaven
and earth who is completely independent of us. This
woman had understood that in the Nazi period in Germany God was small and weak. God was in fact powerless because God had no friends, male or female. God's
spirit had no place to live; God's sun, the sun of
righteousness, did not shine. The God who needs people
in order to come into being was a nobody.

This woman did not look up to heaven in order to be
comforted by an Almighty Father. She looked within
and around herself. She found "that of God," as the
Quakers often say, in herself, the strength for resistance,
the courage for a clear no in a world that is drunk
on the blood of the innocent. And she found another
gift of the Spirit, the help of other brothers and sisters.
She was not alone. She did not submit herself to a God

who was falsely understood as fate. Nor did she consider living without God and in complete assimilation to the values of this world — career, prestige, income. Instead she held firm to the God who is in us as the power of liberation. Her God was small, a minority, laughable, politically suspect and, from a pragmatic viewpoint, unsuccessful. God is practically speaking irrelevant for the great majority precisely because of God's non-interference. But God is (to use an expression of American theologians) no "interventionist," who interferes by intervening, but an "intentionist," who makes the divine will and intention discernible. I could simply say: God dreams us, even today.

But, I hear someone object, doesn't this way of speaking about God only make sense if God embodies some kind of power? If something in our lives changes through and with God? Who is this God who has caused a woman not to let Auschwitz rest, not to let fate be fate, not to give way to the ordinary fatalism of subordination to the wolves that howl the loudest. Does such a God have any kind of power, then, or is this form of divinity as powerless in the face of the forces that control us as any child in Bethlehem? I think the question whether God is the one who holds everything in hand and can intervene or whether God is small under the forces of this world cannot be decided rationally, but rather existentially. "When I had understood Auschwitz, I joined the peace movement." That is to say: I did not rid myself of God like many who had handed over responsibility to God alone; rather I grasped that God needs us in order to realize what was intended in creation. God dreams us, and we should not let God dream alone. In the words of a Latin American song:

> One day the earth will belong to all people
> and the people will be free

as you, God, have willed it
from the very beginning.

This song speaks *to* God, not *about* God. It liberates us from the idol of fate in whose power everything happens simply as it happens. It binds us together with a God who is not the all-powerful conqueror but stands instead on the side of the poor and disadvantaged — a God who is always hidden in the world and wants to become visible.

Nothing can separate us from the love of God, we read in the Letter to the Romans (8:35f.). We do not experience this deepest certainty if we want to wrap ourselves like children in God's mantle and then, when we grow up, believe we don't need God anymore. The world is too cold for us to think that we could live without this mantle. Grace warms us, but it helps us at the same time to knit together on God's mantle.

CHAPTER 2

Images of God

WESTERN tradition has been the bearer of a series of andromorphic images of God, such as king and sovereign, judge and lord, shepherd and father.[1] All these conceptions of the Godhead are to be understood against the background of a tension related to the human capacity for visualization, to the power of religious imagination itself. The two poles of this tension, which runs through the Christian tradition up to the present day, are the veneration of icons and the prohibition of images.

On the one hand, images are dramatizations of life, expressive representations of our wishes and fears. Without imaging life we cannot experience "meaning." Hope cannot manage with mere argument. We need a language that says more than can be justified empirically. The father in heaven, father of all orphans, father of all those whose empirical fathers have long since taken off, is an image of longing to find justice and a home. There are those who have been deprived of their rights — widows, for example, in a patriarchal legal structure; there are the homeless who need a place where they cannot be driven away. "Home," wrote William Faulkner, "is where they have to take you in." That is the productive, liberating, and comforting function of the father image.

The heavenly father stands for this homeland of all people. Black slaves have sung:

Oh, when I get to heaven, I'll walk all about
There's nobody there for to turn me out.

Images like that of the father are used, loved, and honored most by those who are thrown out everywhere and not allowed to run around freely anywhere. I call to mind this God of the blacks, who promises free space, protection, and dignity, because in white middle-class culture the father is often interpreted completely differently — as the great policeman who sees all and knows all, for example — and other experiences hardly come into consideration. In the religious traditions of the poor, images of consolation are passed on, given by the grandmother to the granddaughter. They are also written down, exegeted, subjected to theological reflection. But above all they are fitted into hierarchical structures of power and made into instruments of power. Their inner strength, however, does not seem to me to stem from what the Enlightenment liked to call "clerical deceit" but rather from the need of those who had already always been cheated out of happiness, justice, and honor. They are the ones who need images.

On the other hand, the three great monotheistic religions at least recognize the prohibition against making images of the divine. In Islam this prohibition of images is absolute: only in rugs, which are trodden with feet, may images surface. In Judaism the interior of the Temple is empty, a shrine without content, without statues or relics. The iconoclastic tradition belongs to the oldest stock of the Hebrew Bible. "You shall not make a carved image for yourself nor the likeness of anything in the heavens above, or on the earth below, or in the waters under the earth. You shall not bow down to them or worship them; for I, the Lord your

God, am a jealous god . . ." (Exodus 20:4–5; cf. Deut. 27:15). All notions of God, all pictures of the One whom no eye has seen nor ear heard are rejected again and again, as the story of the golden calf testifies.

This tradition of prohibiting images has been toned down and moderated in Christianity. But it breaks out at certain points in church history over and over again and with religious, indeed iconoclastic fervor. In 726 C.E. the Byzantine Emperor Leo III, named the Isaurian, began a struggle against those who venerated icons. In this conflict, church tradition, devotion, art, even the learned theology of John of Damascus stood on the side of the monks, who lived from the icons, and of the people, who didn't want the icons to be taken away. This conflict between the *ikonolatrai* or *ikonodouloi*, that is, between the venerators of icons and the emperor and his iconoclasts (*ikonoklastai*) flared up frequently in succeeding eras, as in the Reformation. The image-venerating, image-friendly tendency often proceeds from the people, whereas both enlightened reason and religious intensity are inclined to iconoclasm. It is useful even today to keep in mind these different sources of the criticism of certain concepts of divinity: feminist theology is the clearest contemporary expression of the struggle against the ideology of patriarchy — for the sake of the greater divinity. "Therefore I beg of God," says Meister Eckhart, "that he rid me of God." That is a plea for liberation from the prison of a language which is too small for God; today it is a plea for liberation from a God who is no more than a father.

Perhaps no image of God is as ambiguous as that of the father, as easy to misuse for authoritarian religion, as easy to harden into obedience and subjection. Authoritarian religion in Erich Fromm's sense is characterized by three structural elements:

21

recognition of a higher power that holds our fate in
its hands and excludes any self-determination;
submission to the rule of this power, which needs no
moral legitimation such as love or justice;
a deep pessimism about the human person: he or she
is not capable of love or truth, but is a powerless and
meaningless being whose obedience feeds on the very
denial of his or her own strength.[2]

The main virtue in authoritarian religion is obedience,
its cardinal sin rebellion, in contrast to humanitarian
religion, which moves self-actualization and lapses of
the self into center stage.

Authoritarian religion as a type is to be distinguished
from humanitarian religion. The Jewish prophets, the
historical Jesus, early Buddhism, and mystics of most
religions are examples of a nonrepressive religion that
does not rest on a one-sided, asymmetrical dependence
or become realized through internal compulsion. It is
precisely at this point that social-psychological questions
about the symbol of the father come into play. What
does the image of father mean within this distinction?
What relation to the divine does it express?

My involvement with this question has taught me to
look anew at the chasm which exists between the biblical tradition and the history of the corruption of Christianity. Measured by the role of the father in our
contaminated contemporary speech about God, the reti-
cence of the Hebrew Bible with regard to the designation
of God the Father is astonishing. The Exodus tradition,
which forms the crucible of the first biblical image of
God, gets by without "father," as do the creation
accounts. The "God of our fathers" was earlier than
God the Father. The vision at the burning bush, in
which God gives the name "I am that I am," does not
transmit a father theology. "This revelation of the

name," writes Paul Ricoeur, "signifies the annulment of all anthropomorphic conceptions, all forms and shapes, including the form of the father. The name stands against the idol."[3]

There are only about twenty places in the Hebrew Bible where God is designated as father.[4] The father name emerges within the prophetic message with Hosea, Jeremiah, and in Third Isaiah, and always in the context of the prophetically understood future of a new creation. "I said, How gladly would I treat you as a son, giving you a pleasant land, a patrimony fairer than that of any nation! I said, You shall call me Father and never cease to follow me" (Jeremiah 3:19 NEB). It is not a matter here of origin but of the new creation in which the people will no longer be separated from God. "Only those who make this turn [from origin to eschatology] truly know and recognize the father."[5] To recognize the father does not mean to illuminate the mythical origin of the people but to seek the coming kingdom, where "righteousness and peace will kiss each other" (Psalm 85:10 RSV). Precisely because the myth of origin — that of the father — breaks forth with the prophetic message, as do the symbols of origin — land and people — the biblical tradition contains the potential of a radical critique of the patriarchal religious order which excludes the woman from a relationship to the holy: it is idolatry.

This line continues on into the Synoptic Gospels: the kingdom of God, not the heavenly father, is the central message. Jesus stands in the tradition of the economy of justice proclaimed by the prophets. Therefore the father image is to be interpreted from the standpoint of the kingdom of God, not the other way around, against all authoritarian or sentimental religion which uses the authority of the father in order to degrade justice to a powerless dream. "Our Father in the heavens" is not one of flesh and blood but rather the divine figure imagined from the petition for the coming kingdom. If God in the Bible is the liberator from Egyptian slavery and Roman death politics, if the Exodus of the people of Israel and the resurrection of Jesus of Nazareth are the central, remembered, and repeated foundational experiences of faith, then it is from here that our contemporary experiences of God and contaminations of God are to be gauged: What place, then, should the internalized overseer, the policeman who never sleeps, the ruler who controls everything occupy? God can be called "father" in the Bible on the basis of all the other divine concepts which name God's actions: freeing slaves, feeding the hungry, healing the sick, warding off enemies, restoring rights to those deprived of their rights.

Jesus, fully a Jew in this also, labels the relationship between the children and the father in the Sermon on the Mount as one of asking and giving: "Or what man of you, if his son asks him for bread, will give him a stone? Or if he asks for a fish, will give him a serpent? If you then, who are evil, know how to give good gifts to your children, how much more will your Father who is in heaven give good things to those who ask him!" (Matt. 7:9–11 RSV). Asking and giving, in the last consequence giving oneself, is, as Ricoeur has shown, neither an Oedipal nor a servant–lord relationship. It is not the uniqueness of the relationship between God the Father and the only-begotten Son that stands in the center here but rather the universality of God, who relates to all his children like a father (even an evil one), giving, nourishing, bestowing. It is not for the son a matter of snatching away power or life force from the father, and it is not — as in later Christian interpretation with all its sado-masochistic implications — the will of the father to sacrifice the son. It is the will of the father to be father and to bestow life. The right relation of the children to the father is not interpreted as obedience, subjection, breaking of the will, but rather as a trusting petition which is heard. Asking and giving point to the fact that the power of God is only a good, life-loving power when it is shared. The father who is obsessed with his power, watches over it, and will let not let anything be taken from him may be an end product of the social history of Christianity; but it has nothing in common with the use of the word in the Bible.

The most important questions about the dominant theology posed by an emerging feminist theology are directed, iconoclastically, against phallocratic fantasies, against the adoration of power. Why do people venerate a God whose most important quality is power, whose interest is subjection, whose fear is equality? Why worship a being who is addressed as "Lord," whose theologians must testify to his omnipotence because power alone is not enough for him? Why should we honor and love a being who does not transcend the moral level of contemporary culture as shaped by men, but instead establishes it?

A religion which from its origins was oriented toward liberation took on unmistakable traits of patriarchalism when it became rigidified. The origins of Israel's faith, with its emphasis on the liberating God, carries clear marks of equality, indeed of equalizing unequal distribution. The traditions of the sabbath and the year of the sabbath up to the year of jubilee serve to liberate those people who fell into misfortune and then into debtors' slavery; they equalize land ownership anew.

But these tendencies of liberation theology stand over against other tendencies of a hierarchical sort. God is made masculine in a double sense: the matriarchal cults are exterminated and the "other," nature-related, feminine side of God recedes. This masculinization of God, which in Christianity is extremely advanced, as it is

expressed in purely androcentric language, always goes
hand in hand with deification of the male.

I want to explain this criticism within the framework
of my own theological biography: my difficulties with
the great ruler arose in relation to the experience of
Auschwitz. It seemed inconceivable to me to retain love
and omnipotence within the father image. In 1965 I
published my first book, *Christ the Representative: An
Essay in Theology after the "Death of God."*[6] The position
represented there is, in the tradition of Dietrich Bonhoeffer, radically Christocentric. God's self, God as one who
acts and speaks, cannot be experienced. We can hold to
Christ, who is powerless and without dominion, who
has nothing but his love to win us and to save us.
His powerlessness is an inner authority. Not because he
generated, created, or made us are we his, but because
love is his unarmed power, stronger than death.

Jews who went into the gas chamber praying the
Sh'ma Israel (Deut. 6:4–9) were to me a stronger proof
of God than speculations on omnipotence by theologians who seemed to me like the voluble friends of
Job. Independently of Auschwitz, as if what happened
there did not affect them, they proclaimed their God as
dominating and regulating everything.

My difficulties with the father, begetter, ruler, and
controller of history deepened as I came to understand
more precisely what it meant to be born as a woman,
(that is, in the language of the tradition, "defective")
and to live in a sexist society. How could I will that
power be the central category of my life? How could I
worship a God who is no more than a man?

In this process it became clearer to me that every
identification with the aggressor, with the ruler, with
the violator is the worst misfortune that can befall a
woman. Even the milder side of this lord, which is
expressed with the father symbol, does not have the

same fascination for those who can never become a father. Even the power which is replaced by mercy, even the most benevolent father, is no solution to the problem. A benevolent slaveholder can be loved and venerated by his slaves; female devotion has to a large extent been Uncle Tom devotion. But submission to the roles defined socially as "feminine" and obedience to God, who supposedly set the rules in nature, destroy women's possibilities of becoming a human being. An omnipotent (and unbiblical) father cannot free us from the history of my people and from the sexism of a dominant culture. Can the symbol "father" still represent in any way what we mean by the word "God"?

When it is understood that we can speak only symbolically about God, every symbol that sets itself up as absolute must be relativized. We cannot live without symbols, but we must relativize them and surpass them iconoclastically. God in fact transcends our speech about God, but only when we do not lock God into prisons of symbols. Feminist theology does not deny that "father" is *one* mode of speaking about God, but when we are forced to make it the only mode, the symbol becomes God's prison. All the other symbol words which people have used to express their experience of God are thus repressed by means of this obligatory language or else pushed down to a lower level on the hierarchy.

Pope John Paul I noted, in a remark that has drawn a lot of attention, that God is at least as much a mother as a father. From a practical religious standpoint we are still far behind in this relativizing of symbolic language. After a worship service which we began with the words "In the name of the Father and the Mother, of the Son and the Holy Spirit," there was a heated discussion on whether one may speak thus. The change of liturgical, sacralized language is a step out of the prison and is therefore experienced as a threat. As a blessing, four women said together: "May God bless you and protect you. May she lift up her countenance over you and give you peace."[7]

These are examples of groping attempts being made everywhere today where women are becoming conscious of their situation. The desire for another image of God, other symbols and other hopes, is important for those who need another God because they have been insulted, humiliated, and disgusted by the culture in which we live.

The relativizing of a symbol for God used as an absolute, as represented by "father," is a minimal demand in this context. There are other symbols for God: keeping within the use of familial language, we can say "mother" or "sister" to her. To me symbols from the natural world, with their non-authoritarian qualities, are clearer yet. To be free of images of dominance, theological language can go back to the mystical tradition. "Wellspring of all good things," "living wind," "water of life," "light," are symbols of God without authority or power and without a chauvinistic flavor.

Recognition of a "higher power," the adoration of lordship, the denial of one's own strength, these have no place in mystical devotion. The lord–servant relationship was often expressly criticized in mysticism, but above all it was surpassed by creative use of language. Religion here is the sensation of being one with the whole, of belonging, not of subjection. People do not honor God because of God's power and lordship; rather they "submerge" themselves in God's love, which is "ground," "depth," "ocean." Mother- and nature-symbols are preferred where the relationship to God does not demand obedience but union, where no distant Other requires sacrifice and self-denial, but where

28

instead agreement and oneness with the Living One become the theme of religion. Solidarity will then replace obedience as the most important virtue.

Are there elements in the father symbol for God that are indispensable for a liberating theology? Does the personal mode of referring to God take precedence over other possible symbols? Is the connection between God and Father indissoluble? Do we need a Thou construed as Father to be the Other for humans?

In patriarchal culture the father represents the dependence of the individual. It is a biological given in the fact of being engendered and in the long dependence of the young person, who must be cared for and protected. But does our long childhood justify a religious language that is essentially oriented to the parent–child relationship? And does not the removal of the mother from this relationship — as if it were the father and he alone who guarantees creation, generation, and survival — sharpen the authoritarian element even further?

The image of the father in agrarian patriarchal cultures is oriented toward the functions of the head of the household, who represents certain legal, religious, pedagogical, and economic powers. He is judge, priest, teacher, and he controls the means of production. When the accumulation of biological and sociological power roles is divided into separate occupations and increasingly belongs to an incomprehensible past, the corresponding religious superstructure loses its foundation. Does the father image still have any liberating function?

A central question of every feminist philosophical or theological discussion is that concerning the relationship between dependence and independence for women. Is independence a word of liberation, a central value that women discover for themselves? Or are there dependencies which are not to be denied? Is it good to make oneself emotionally independent, or does that only get us to where the men are, with their superficial ties, which the ideologized independence of the male hero is not allowed to touch? What does it mean anthropologically to be dependent? And what does it mean for our relationship to nature, to work, in society? The field of this discussion within feminism is also the field of theological decisions. Is dependence nothing more than a repressive inheritance, or does it belong to our createdness? I tend to the second statement and have therefore no difficulty holding on to the religious symbols "father" and "mother."

We did not make or design ourselves or position ourselves historically and geographically. The context of our life knows a before and an after, to which we stand in relation and from which we cannot separate ourselves without harm. Ontologically we are not alone. There is, we must believe, a unity to the world, a wholeness, a goal. Does not the talk about God as father of the living express precisely this dependency as connectedness, as standing in relation? In the words of Simon Dach (1605–1659), as known through one of the hymns of Johann Sebastian Bach,

> I am, O Lord, within thy might,
> 'tis thou hast brought me to the light,
> and you preserve for me my life,
> and you know the number of my moons,
> and when I to this vale of gloom
> again must say my last good night.
> Where, how, and when I am to die,
> you know, O Father, more than I.

At the beginning of this strophe, God is called "Lord," at the end "Father": what kind of process leads from the first to the second concept? The power of the Lord who is finally called "Father," is expressed here with precision: it is generative and life-creating, it is the power that sustains life and that ends life. Our being born and our dying do not lie in our hands. To call God father means that life and death are not handed over to a vitalistic randomness, to say nothing of technological control. To regard the world as a creation means to regard it as willed, as planned, as "good." If talk of God as father helps us not just to accept our dependence as a remnant of earth to be overcome but to affirm it and to accept our finitude and creaturehood, then there is no basis for objecting to this way of speaking.

Familial symbols of God, the talk of God our Father and God our Mother, can have a liberating effect not because they alleviate the dehumanizing, oppressive characteristics of patriarchy but because they bind us to nature and to the human family. Talk of God as father is no longer exploited sociologically in order to establish roles and reinforce false dependencies; it is not used in order to keep us children forever. Rather it makes us capable of trusting in the life which goes beyond our own life span. It also creates trust in Brother Death.

The feminist criticism represented here concerning the concept of God as father is internal to the Christian tradition. The religious portion of the women's movement is currently "overthrowing" the image of father — but not in the interest of an imageless space without religious connections. The picture of the heavenly father is instead being criticized with the aim of a deeper, more serious religiosity. "Our Mother in Heaven" and "Goddess" are emerging. But the iconoclastic women are not overthrowing God the Father for the sake of an illusion of being free of images.

Other feminists understand themselves as post-Christian and conceive of themselves as engaged in a sometimes quiet, sometimes noisy exodus from the tradition they regard as hopelessly patriarchal. The "overthrow of the gods," understood as depriving the fathers of their power both within social history and in religious symbolism, is thus believed to be and is promoted as a liberating event.[8]

For the feminism of liberation theology, for which I speak here, it is questionable whether a rationally based criticism of the authoritarian conception of God, as it is expressed in the father symbol, is sufficient. Or whether the real idols which rule over us are only endorsed by abolishing that for which the "father" was a symbol. Or whether withdrawal into imagelessness will not already give rise in the next generation, growing up tradition-"free," to emptiness, helplessness, and adaptation.

Authority and subjection can indeed be sanctioned religiously in the father image, but that says nothing about the naked continuation of the same social structures in a post-religious space. In order for industrialism to function today, patriarchal hierarchy has to be dismantled; personal authority has been replaced by objective constraints, and subjection functions marvellously, even without a father. The idea of a creator, father and sustainer of life, that is, the conception of the holiness of life, has become rather dysfunctional; it may possibly disturb the smooth process of subjection under technocracy.

At the beginning of the European peace movement, the Reformed Church of the Netherlands asserted that the production, testing, and storage of atomic bombs was a sin, namely blasphemy against "Father, Son and Spirit." Such tiny disturbances, as they proceed in many places of the world from churches and synagogues — from organized religion, therefore — are signs of hope. The "overthrow of the gods" does not yet make us free. It is perhaps only a more efficient reorganization of the powers and forces under which we live, in the shadow of two atomic bombs — one for the end of life and nuclear winter and the other for its beginning manipulated through genetic engineering. Both processes, creating life and ending it, work toward taking back creation. "To undo creation" is their goal.[9] Both processes stem from the same intellectual structure, namely the patriarchy which subjects nature to itself and as "science" knows no limits and takes a neutral stance with regard to questions about humanness. The most dangerous, repressive traits of the old God — his omnipotence and his demand for absolute submission — are transferred over to the new idols, only they have better methods of implementing them. The humanizing traits of the father image — his mercy and his justice — were not secularized along with the others and got lost, except with those minorities who resist.

Why overthrow the gods? In whose interest? Is the computer a better god? The bases of the scientific worldview with their technological imperialism no longer need a father symbol in order to legitimize their racism, their animosity toward women, and their total war against the natural foundations of life.

Doing away with the Father God does not mean that the male is no longer idolized. The concept of humans as made in the image of machines, and the exclusion or even destruction of those who do not behave like machines and let themselves be exploited, has already de facto won. I suspect that scientists for the most part have not really taken cognizance of either Auschwitz or Hiroshima. The overthrow of the (ambiguous) gods is followed by the lordship of Moloch. The masculinization of God and the suppression of the female side of God are followed by the deification of the male — in the technocracy. "Technically we are capable of *everything*," said General Abrahamsson, a high functionary of the military-scientific complex responsible for the military utilization of space (SDI).[10] That is more than the normal arrogance of power, more even than visions of omnipotence.

The end of patriarchal religion, which we are experiencing, has a liberating character only if it calls us into resistance. The question posed to organized religion is not how much the Father can be salvaged but how much power of resistance we can receive from God, the Ground of Life, and how long reform is still possible. At the end of the patriarchal era of religion other images of God are emerging among us.

Some of the rabbinic mystics believed concerning the time of exile that, while the Father had turned his face away from Israel in anger, nevertheless the *Shekinah* of God, God's indwelling, remained among the people. "Each Shabbat celebration is seen as a mystical connubial embrace of God with his *Shekinah*, anticipating the final reuniting of God with creation in the messianic age. The exile of Israel from the land is seen ultimately as an exile within God, divorcing the masculine from the feminine 'side' of God."[11] In these speculations the transcendence of God is perceived as masculine and God's immanence as feminine. Perhaps the *Shekinah*, God's presence which accompanies the people into exile, is the form of God which reveals the most to us about God today.

NOTES

1. This text first appeared in Werner Faulstich and Gunter E. Grimm, eds., *Sturz der Götter? Vaterbilder in Literatur, Medien und Kultur des 20. Jahrhunderts* (Frankfurt, 1988). The usual expression, "anthropomorphic," presumes the usual, mistaken identification of human being with the male! In this chapter I employ masculine pronouns when referring to this andromorphic-imaged God.

2. Cf. Erich Fromm, *Psychoanalysis and Religion* (New Haven, Conn.: Yale University Press, 1950).

3. Paul Ricoeur, "Die Vatergestalt — vom Phantasiebild zum

Symbol", in *Hermeneutik und Psychoanalyse: Der Konflikt der Interpretationen II.* (Munich 1974), 337.

4. Cf. Joachim Jeremias, *The Prayers of Jesus* (Philadelphia: Fortress Press, 1978) 12.

5. Paul Ricoeur, "Die Vatergestalt," 341.

6. Dorothee Soelle, *Christ the Representative: An Essay in Theology after the "Death of God"* (Philadelphia: Fortress Press, 1967). In German: *Stellvertretung: Ein Kapitel Theologie nach dem "Tode Gottes"* (Kreuz Verlag, 1965).

7. Dorothee Soelle, "Fatherhood, Power, and Barbarism," *The Window of Vulnerability: A Political Spirituality*, trans. Linda M. Maloney (Minneapolis: Fortress Press, 1990), 85–92.

8. Mary Daly, *Beyond God the Father: Toward a Philosophy of Women's Liberation* (Boston: Beacon Press, 1973).

9. Dorothee Soelle with Shirley A. Cloyes, *To Work and to Love: A Theology of Creation* (Philadelphia: Fortress Press, 1984), 3.

10. Dorothee Soelle, *Ein Volk ohne Vision geht zugrunde* (Wuppertal, 1986), 100ff.

11. Rosemary Radford Ruether, "The Female Nature of God: A Problem in Contemporary Religious Life," in Johannes-Baptist Metz and Edward Schillebeeckx, eds., *God as Father?* (Concilium: Religion in the Eighties; Edinburgh: T. & T. Clark, 1981), 63.

Chapter 3

Names of God

IF I WERE to summarize the position of feminist theology after twenty-five years, it would be that patriarchy in its talk about God misses the transcendence of God. If God is only called "he," then God is thought of as too small. That which actually should be expressed cannot really be said in sexist language that ignores half of humanity. The concept of the natural inferiority of women and the legitimation of their subjection, which they like to present theologically as a subjection given in creation, is — for both sexes, by the way — one of the greatest obstacles on the long path to becoming fully human. "Anatomy is destiny," said Freud, unaware of how the misogynous substance of this sentence strikes back at those who utter it, institutionalize it, and live it, as if freedom, strength of ego, and humanization were possibly only for a part of humanity and at the cost of the other part, which by nature remains unfree.

A citation from the writings of the church father Jerome indicates the ideological continuity: "As long as the woman lives for giving birth and having children, there remains the same difference between her and the man as between body and soul; if, however, she wants to serve Christ more than the world, she will cease to be woman and will be called 'man' because we desire that all be lifted to perfect manhood."[1] The understanding of the creator God expressed here verifies my opening thesis. According to this tradition, God created nothing but the man, and this creature man is incapable of thinking the other unless as a usable object. If God is not more than a male, then the male is God. Sexism is heresy, is contrary to Scripture (Genesis 1:27; Exodus 2:14), and makes a phallic idol out of God. The reciprocal relationship that exists between the patriarchal image of God and the male positions of power in church and society can be observed wherever either of the two pillars Father-God or masculine power is shaken within organized religion.

Just as a name does not suffice for a human being, likewise for God also — a name, as something of a familial symbol, is misleading. The divine must be understood in the categories of a relationship of opposites which is in itself harmonious and dynamic: present and hidden, powerful and helpless, suffering and comforting, mother and father, punishing and saving. Every attempt to name God with a word that excludes, and to make the father in Jesus' "Our Father" into a guarantor of unchanging language, is an attack on this God, who is thereby controlled and integrated into the realm of things at one's disposal. "I will be who I will be" is an attempt to repudiate the dominant idolatry by turning language around.

God exceeds God, as the process theologians say. As with every good theological statement, this too has a critical, exclusionary sense, which then reads: A God who does not exceed God is not God. God imprisoned in a certain language, limited by certain definitions, known by names that have established certain socio-cultural forms of control, is not God but becomes instead a religious ideology. Symbols, as for instance that of the omnipotence of God, tell me more about the projections and wishes of the men who use them than about God.

Names can become God's prison. I, for example, still hear Adolf Hitler bellowing whenever I read the expression "the All-Powerful."

Feminist theology arises, as does every liberation theology, from the experience of being wounded. It grows from the destruction inflicted on the lives of women, whether conceived in economic, political, social, intellectual, or psychic terms. It makes mutilations visible. It arises among women who perceive their situation and take common steps to change it, breaking out of the conventions and forms of the dominant theology and its pact with power. The pact which is made there tenders a cultural task for the church which contradicts its mission and its tradition: the church is supposed to make the victims of our situation invisible; and if this isn't possible, at least the causes of the misery should remain fatefully uncertain. Preachers may tell of Mary and Joseph but should not know the particular homeless in our own cities. They expound on the story of the paralytic and his friends, but whether those suffering from AIDS have friends, they don't know. They mention the "hungry," but the feminization of poverty remains outside of their horizon.

In view of the real suffering of women, the theology and devotional practices of churches show up as strangely blind and ignorant. Among feminist women who have begun to reflect from the perspective of their wounds, there has spread astonishment concerning the dispassionate abstractness of masculine theology, boredom with biblical exegesis removed from experience and praxis, and revulsion against spiritless masculine administration within the institution. "Therefore I ask God," writes Meister Eckhart, "to rid me of God." That is no heresy but rather the petition for liberation from the prison of a language which is too small for God.

Therefore I ask God my Mother — so I understand Eckhart today — to rid me of the God of men.

The issue is more than about "feminine aspects in God," to which enlightened men today readily admit. Their talk disturbs me, as if God were intrinsically and primarily masculine and as if those feminine elements which had been kept hidden must now be brought out as a supplement. According to this scheme of thought, the feminine lies hidden in God as the child is known to lie hidden in the man. But it is not sufficient to want to discover the yet unknown feminine in the well-known masculine God; within the framework of this deconstruction, the feminist critique has not yet gone far enough. Wouldn't we with equal justification have to discover the negroid traits and the youthful elements in God in order finally to get rid of the old white man in heaven? Our inner difficulty does not lie in the more or less false pictures of God which have been handed down to us, and we cannot overcome the spirit-less desolation in which we live by setting up statues of goddesses or pictures of matriarchy in the temples that have been emptied. We are not lacking in pictures but in identifiable experiences of God. Caught in a strait-jacket of masculine authoritarian language, we have been rendered incapable of identifying the secret of life which we call God as something experienced.

I do not mean that people experience God less today than in earlier times. God's presence and absence are given to us, too, in jubilation and desperation and some-times even in the puzzling mixture of both. Life itself is so permeated with this quality that we call God that we cannot avoid feeding on it and hungering after it. Only we often don't know that because we have been rend-ered incapable of speaking. We do not dare connect that which in fact deserves to be called an "experience of God" with the God of the religion administered by men.

The priests and theologians have talked so long that we have become mute. They have locked God up in Bible and liturgy instead of using Bible and liturgy as eye-glasses for understanding our everyday lives.

While in reality God is present and recognizable at many places in our lives, we lack the language to name God. The power of trivialization which especially harms women convinces us that what we experience is "nothing but" technological necessity, the result of causes which are beyond our control, emotional oversti-mulation, etc. The know-it-all attitude and insensitivity of this "nothing but" diminishes the spirit, sensibilities, and fantasies of women. We have been trained to trivial-ize everyday life instead of sanctifying it. Nothing which affects us is protected from trivialization. At the same time the indifferent "nothing but" expresses a loss of self-respect. We don't know that when the gospel speaks of a hemorrhaging or crippled woman, it refers to us normal, menstruating or aging women, for example. The God-from-above which religion made into a fetish has truncated our lives from their connection to God.

I am reminded of hearing a report from a young woman about the events at Greenham Common, where women regularly met in vigil against Britain's nuclear-missile deployment. While she spoke I saw in the light of the searchlights the faces of the unarmed women in front of me. But more precisely I saw the face of God, about which the Bible speaks, shining in them. Later I wrote a poem with the title "What Mary is telling":

> Two circles in Greenham Common
> one beaming brighter within
> there the silos were built
> and the dogs trained
> and the machine guns finished

and outside in the dark
stood forty thousand women

They had written letters
they hung on the fence
a midwife tacked up her diploma
because she helps to bring forth life
therefore she remains standing here
in front of the bunkers of power
and the agitated dogs
howl in the light of searchlights.

These liturgies of resistance
like Moses at the burning bush
we stand before fences and walls
no, I wept not only out of fear
out of shame and sorrow
it was naked life itself
our vulnerable short life
naked and finally visible.

That too is a text about God, but probably the word
"God" would lead further away from God, because the
word is occupied by the language of the patriarchate
and its worship of power. Within the framework of this
occupation the Bible and liturgy can no longer do that
for which they are intended, namely to make the
mystery of God visible also for us, *pro nobis*. The dominant theology has given both of these an authoritarian
unapproachability, so that people can no longer express
their deepest experiences in the language of God and
cannot share them with others. Without form, without
language, the experiences die; they are not appropriated.
Language not only depicts what is, it also restores to
consciousness what has been experienced. In this sense
successful God language is a steady knocking on the
door of memory. It says, "Do you not know more? . . .

Just remember . . . It was like this for you too." At the same time it is an interpretation of reality that we cannot do without, an emphatic interpretation that protects us from trivialization of ourselves. Those women who came to awareness of their strength within the peace movement or other liberation movements would no longer tolerate such trivializing phraseology as "I as an individual cannot do anything anyway." They know that they are bearers of life. "We know that we have come from death into life, for we love the sisters" (1 John 3:14). This sentence from the First Letter of John articulates the experience of resistance among Christian minorities, then as today.

But is this presupposition really correct? Do these wonderful and painful experiences and afflictions from God exist? Do we really experience that God is nearer to me than I am to myself? I remember a feminist group in New York where we tried to speak of our own religious experiences. A woman who has been my friend ever since that day reported on the destructive and humiliating experiences of her Christian socialization. Then she paused and spoke about her sexual experience, which showed her for the first time what might be meant by the word "God" — that oceanic feeling of not being separate from anything or hindered by anything, the happiness of being one with everything living, the ecstasy in which the old "I" is abandoned and I am new and different. Goethe spoke once of the "freshness of the nights of love, which begot you as you begot." That is expressed in male language, but the experience of being born where we conceive and give birth, of not being able to separate the passive and active experiencing and enduring, of being neither the one acting nor the one being acted upon, is rooted in women's experience. The language of religion, by which I do not mean the stolen language in which a male God ordains and imperial power radiates forth, is the language of mysticism: I am completely and utterly in God, I cannot fall out of God, I am imperishable. "Who shall separate us from the love of God?" we can then ask with Paul the mystic; "neither death nor life, height nor depth, neither present nor future" (Romans 8:35 and 38).

I would like to relate one more example, one of the many experiences of being abandoned by God. In November 1983 the German Parliament in Bonn decided to agree to the stationing of medium-range missiles. I was on the street in Bonn with many friends, both male and female. It was a slap in the face for us after years of work in persuasion and liberation, in which we had spent time, energy, and money. It was a humiliation for democracy, for the great majority of the people rejected the weapons of mass destruction. It was an assault on the truth with the argument that first-strike weapons should ostensibly serve for "defense." I was supposed to give a talk and I didn't know what to say. Many of us who were demonstrating were drenched by water cannons and driven through the streets by the police. Why have you abandoned us, God, I thought. Why do you not show your face? Why do you not prepare us a "table in the presence of our enemies" (Psalm 23) rather than inviting those who do not ask for you to a banquet? I no longer know what I said in that dark night, but one sentence was, "Truth will make us free," an oath of God that truth will not always remain buried under lies. Many regarded what I said as a prayer, even though I hardly used religious vocabulary. In any case this prayer was not directed to an authoritarian power-up-above, who might have forced a different decision with lightning, thunder, supernatural intervention, or magical appearances. The God to whom this prayer went was sad like us, small like us, without bank accounts or bombs as backing, exactly like us. Yet God was with us in this night. In our godforsaken state we lacked God, and this lack, this hunger for a single piece of edible bread in Bonn was with us. The Regent, Sovereign, All-powerful Potentate did not, indeed could not, help us. But the God of defeat and of pain, the God of Golgotha, was with us.

Praesentia Dei — in the fullness of being-in-God and in the emptiness of abandonment — those are foundational experiences which without God-language remain mute and helpless, which we then cannot share and which cannot change us. God-language makes us capable of speech, helps us in communicating that on which it depends, and it creates in us again and again "the new heart and a new and certain spirit" (Psalm 51:12).

The Christian feminist movement ties into everyday experiences, and even its reflective aspect, called feminist theology, has to fasten onto the everyday experience of women. The word "experience," meanwhile, has become fashionable, and unfortunately, in the even more misused word *Selbsterfahrung*, or self-experience, even the last vestige of going away and traveling into the world has been lost.[2] I find the insistence on experience among women often to be childish and highly subjective. Yet this longing for a lived, existential religion has in its helplessness so much more justification than the frozen academic wisdom of a theology which does not bother with the context of those living today. A linguistic search for God has gotten started, and it is being carried out by those who had lost their language, the women. It is not a matter of supplementing existing theology, for what supplement should be added to the stones it mainly offers? Feminist theology is a cry for bread.

It is no accident that its first and still most widespread form is liturgy. Prayers, songs, dance and bodily move-

ment, group Bible discussions, "sister celebrations" are
the forms of expression of this search for an existential
God-language. To learn to speak to God is more important in this than to speak about God. There is a consensus
that the new language does not need to be gender-
exclusive. There is controversy on whether the "Goddess" or similar concepts taken mainly from matriarchal
culture, like the Great Mother, are productive and liberating or whether with them, as I think, the search is
broken off too quickly and we do not carry out Eckhart's
leave-taking from God. Is not parental symbolism in
many respects powerless, because it can indeed express
protection and security, but not the Godhead who goes
with us out of Egypt, not liberation. Mary Daly once
called attention to the fact that a noun is not the appro-
priate type of word for speaking about God. "Why not
a verb — the most active and dynamic of all? ... The
anthropomorphic symbols for God may be intended to
convey personality, but they fail to convey that God is
Be-ing. Women now who are experiencing the shock of
nonbeing and the surge of self-affirmation against this
are inclined to perceive transcendence as the Verb in
which we participate — live, move, and have our
being."[3]

How then are we to think of the relation to transcendence? What power belongs to God, the source and goal
of all life? And what is our relation to this power? Are
relationships between God and human beings which are
interpreted as a power struggle (in the sense of an Oedipal conflict) and which have led to the removal of old
authority, relevant at all? God's impotence in the world
is so obvious; scientific replacement of creation through
a second, better one is only an example that shows how
helpless the old man in heaven is. That God is all-
powerful and we are impotent creatures, for which the
Bible often uses the image of "worm," is no longer

tenable. This theology no longer corresponds to the technology of atom-splitting and genetic engineering, and it
is morally unacceptable. The God-question is decided
according to our understanding of power. Can we think
of power as one-sidedly masculine, as command, physi-
cal superiority, hierarchical order, control of the higher
over the lower? Do we experience God as a coercive
authority, or are there other forms of experiencing God?

Carter Heyward, one of the leading voices of systematic theology between Christianity and post-Christianity,
speaks of God the "power-in-relationship" which lets
us take part in the power of life.[4] In fact God is power,
but precisely not the relationless, self-sufficient power of
the ruler who also uses force when necessary. Modernity
has given its answer to this authoritarian God: it has
made him superfluous. He no longer has a role to play.
He is not scientifically applicable. But is the authoritarian male God all that has been meant within the
Jewish and Christian traditions by the title "God"? What
happens with these other traditions, and how do they
relate to the scientific model of control?

I think that the point of departure of feminist theology
cannot be limited to the criticism of sexist religion and
its institutions. We need a comprehensive critique of
male scientific understanding, of its goals, which are
accepted unquestioningly, and its imperial methods, but
above all of its ethics, which largely functions as a mere
rhetoric of legitimation. Feminist theology participates
in this huge task insofar as it practices an alternative
"God-thinking" which asks the power question anew
and frees it from the authoritarian model of thinking
about the "wholly other" God as ruler. What power,
then, does a Godhead have that neither determines bat-
tles nor protects against ecological or economic catastrophes? Living in a violent culture, in which barbaric
institutions like the military still enjoy legitimacy and

respect, it is nearly impossible for us to think about, even to imagine power that is without force yet can convert and change. We do not know what love could be; for a long time it has only been allowed to run free within a private zoo.

We cannot conceive of God and have no language for God because our concepts of power, mastery, strength, and energy stem, now as before, from the Babylon in which we live. They are all contaminated with violence. We have all grown up under a patriarchal-authoritarian religion or its effects and its substitute in the form of faith in science. Societal mechanisms of coercion have formed our thinking and destroyed our feeling, as for example the human ability to feel sympathy. From women in particular I hear again and again the most godless statement of everyday life, namely, "We cannot do anything about it." And so we cooperate with open eyes in poisoning the water of our grandchildren and dismissing the radiated children of Chernobyl. Unresisting submission to the force that does not allow justice in trade relations, that builds peace on the basis of militarism, and that further destroys or replaces creation has two roots. One is patriarchal Christianity, which is fixated on authority: the authoritarian God is still implored helplessly in the expectation that sometime he will yet intervene. The other root of subjection is the post-religious belief in male science — no longer understood humanistically — which governs over those subjected impotently to it in the manner of an ancient god of fate. The old God can at most represent a kind of protection from catastrophes for true believers, as Christian fundamentalism imagines; he does not have liberating qualities.

The question of feminist liberation theology is not, "Does God exist?" but rather, "Does God occur also among us?" In the process of becoming conscious, on the path out of socially imposed nonbeing, the question whether we need God is excavated from the rubble of tradition. I often have the impression that the longing to transcend actual circumstances is clearest in the fear and desperation of women. It is futile to pursue theology if we do not approach this complicated Brechtian "use" of God. (Herr K. in Bertold Brecht's Keuner stories answers the question whether he believes in God with the counterquestion whether anything would change thereby.) The assurance of divinity is *used* when it rescues us and places our feet on wide open spaces. Without the God-within-us, this God-above-us hardens into a fetish who willed Auschwitz. Here as well as among those who still happily prepare for atomic war because God holds everything in his hands anyway, *Gott* and *Abgott* — to express myself in Reformation terms — coincide completely. They have become indistinguishable. What is worshipped is power, the phallic bull, often called God. His is the power; we are powerless. The more transcendent, the more divine. To overcome such objectified transcendence is the task of a liberating theology. Objectified transcendence represents the God who can be nothing other than a Superman, who thus acts independently, untouchably, and full of power. The claims of absoluteness concerning God — "his" omnipotence, omniscience, omnipresence, all three "omnis" — express the fatal imperialistic tendency of theology, namely the power of the ruler.[5]

In feminist theology, therefore, the issue is not about exchanging pronouns but about another way of thinking of transcendence. Transcendence is no longer to be understood as being independent of everything and ruling over everything else, but rather as being bound up in the web of life. Goethe says in his aphorisms about love: "Voluntary dependence, the most beautiful state, and how would it be possible without love?" God

49

is no less voluntarily dependent than all of us can be through love. That means that we move from God-above-us to God-within-us and overcome false transcendence hierarchically conceived. We must approach mysticism, which comes closest to overcoming the hierarchical masculine conception of God — a mysticism, to be sure, in which the thirst for real liberation does not lead to drowning in the sea of unconsciousness.

According to a sentence of Jacob Boehme, God is "the Nothing that wants to become everything." The actually experienced, powerless Nothing of the injured life with which feminist liberation theology begins, is not redeemed from the outside. For us also, "no higher Being, no God or emperor or tribunal" is present, but there is an integration into the sisterly ground of the living. The mystical certainty that nothing can separate us from the love of God grows when we ourselves become one with love by placing ourselves, freely and without guarantee of success, on the side of love.

NOTES

1. Jerome's "Commentary on Ephesians," *Patrologia Latina* 26, 531ff.
2. [Translator's note: The word *Erfahrung*, which I translate as "experience," has as its stem the German word for "ride, drive, go"; *Selbsterfahrung*, or experience of the self, has no connotation of movement.]
3. Mary Daly, *Beyond God the Father: Toward a Philosophy of Women's Liberation* (Boston: Beacon Press, 1973) 33–34.
4. Isabel Carter Heyward, *The Redemption of God: A Theology of Mutual Relation* (Lanham, Md.: University Press of America, 1982).
5. Cf. Dorothee Soelle, *Thinking about God: An Introduction to Theology* (London: SCM Press; Philadelphia: Trinity Press International, 1990).

CHAPTER 4

The Unknown God

The same night he arose and took his two wives, his two maids, and his eleven children, and crossed the ford of the Jabbok. He took them and sent them across the stream, and likewise everything that he had. And Jacob was left alone; and a man wrestled with him until the breaking of the day. When the man saw that he did not prevail against Jacob, he touched the hollow of his thigh; and Jacob's thigh was put out of joint as he wrestled with him. Then he said, "Let me go, for the day is breaking." But Jacob said, "I will not let you go, unless you bless me." And he said to him, "What is your name?" And he said, "Jacob." Then he said, "Your name shall no more be called Jacob, but Israel, for you have striven with God and with men, and have prevailed." Then Jacob asked him, "Tell me, I pray, your name." But he said, "Why is it that you ask my name?" And there he blessed him. So Jacob called the name of the place Peniel, saying, "For I have seen God face to face, and yet my life is preserved." The sun rose upon him as he passed Penuel, limping because of his thigh.

— Genesis 32:22–31 (RSV)

IF WE understand ourselves as standing in the great tradition of the history of religions that begins with Israel, and if we are "Israel of the true sort, produced from the Spirit,"[1] we should rip out of our thoughts even the faintest shadow of anti-Judaism which may lie within this formulation. As if we had robbed the Jews of their spiritual heritage, suppressed them, and expelled them from what was and is their history, their identity, indeed their God. For we were only later drawn in as additional members of this covenant, which was often betrayed but never terminated. If we are and want to be Israel of the true sort, then we share in the faith of Abraham, Isaac, and Jacob up to the present day. We sing, "Blessed is the one who looks only to Jacob's God and salvation" (*EKG* 248) or "Blessed, yea blessed be the one whose help is the God of Jacob" (*EKG* 258, 3).

Who then is the God of Jacob? Who assaults Jacob? Who blesses him? In reading commentaries, it struck me that most commentators are more interested in the question, "Who is Jacob?" They integrate the puzzling story into his life experiences, probe his bright and his dark sides, his changing relationships to others and to himself, his name as one who grabs the heel, as deceiver, and then finally as a struggler with God.

I have gladly appropriated that, mainly from Elie Wiesel, but the more I grappled with the text, the more I was fascinated by the question, "Who is God in this story?" Not as if the question, "Who is Jacob?" could be detached from this other one, but I caught myself feeling that Jacob isn't so interesting to me because I am already Jacob. I already know these transitions of life in which we must indeed cross over a river. I remember these rites of passage in my life — for example, the day I was expelled from childhood. I remember the enormous difficulties I had with becoming an adult; that was an assault, too, by the trivial, by the spirit of everyday life which brutally deflects our deeds and dreams. And quite naturally today I have deep anxieties in facing the dark river before me: growing old, being left alone, accepting this frailty which slowly crawls up within me.

So I do not seek out Jacob in the story: I *am* already

Jacob. I seek out the other one, the one who assaults and wants to kill; I seek the one who blesses. I would like to learn something from Jacob about God. But that is expressed too modestly: What should it mean really, to learn something "about God," as if God were an object of my curiosity? I am not interested in Jacob but rather in his goal, his abyss. "I will not let you go" – I do not want to cite this sentence, I want to act on it.

Who is this God of Jacob? Who assaults and who blesses? I have written down the words which appear in the commentaries about the one who struggles there through the night with Jacob: the stranger, the nighttime visitor, the demon afraid of the light, the ghost, the spirit who robs and murders, the aggressor, the enemy. In the rabbinic commentaries there appear the words "shepherd," "magician," "wise man," or "bandit." Most interpreters have, to be sure, agreed on "angel," and our story has entered the visual arts, from Rembrandt to Chagall and Herbert Falken, as well as literature, under the title "Jacob wrestling with the angel." Jacob's struggle is a contest with an angel and to that extent holds a middle ground between the devil and God, taking up traits of both. So once again: Who assaults Jacob, who blesses him?

> Each of us wrestles with God
> let us stand by that
> even if we are defeated
> and put out of joint
> each of us wrestles with God
> who waits to be used
> A struggle waits for us.

In thinking about being assaulted, I am reminded of my friend Lore, who lives in Düsseldorf. Perhaps the Rhine bridge there is a ford over the Jabbok. My friend, an exceptionally gifted person with an arrestingly bright, clear rational capacity, was for years the director of a training college. Last summer she had to endure something that I would like to describe with the words of our story: someone wrestled with her and assaulted her defenseless soul.

For months Lore has been in the closed ward of a psychiatric hospital. Many nights she has screamed all night long. She has overturned the carts of cleaning women; she trampled on her glasses — the instrument through which she, in reading, sees the world. She begged me, "Get me out of here." Lore has many and reliable friends. She draws a good pension — but she is as alone as Jacob after he shipped family and possessions — our barricades against unhappiness — ahead of him. She was assaulted, as if the nighttime attacker had sought out my friend in order to show her his power. Her illness broke out anew, by the way, when in the United States her purse with her essential antidepressant medication was stolen.

Assaults, attacks, threats, and the nameless anxieties of the mentally ill — when will the tormentor leave her alone? When will day break? And will she perceive the struggle which is destroying her as a blessing? Is it conceivable for her to hold her ground against the misfortune befalling her, to resist it with so much love of life that it is transformed? "For those who love God," Paul says in the Letter to the Romans, "all things must work for the best" (Romans 8:28). Everything, really? Including sickness of the soul and the spirit? Including destruction?

Jacob must have believed something like this. Otherwise his strength and his wrestling cannot be explained, and above all not the archaic stipulation which he puts to his attacker. "I will not let go of you unless you give me a portion of your power."

One of the finest aspects of the story in my view is

that after Jacob had struggled all night he was in the end not happy to let go of the mysterious guest. He does not let him breathe freely. *Survivre n'est past vivre.* Survival is not sufficient. Jacob wants more; with and in spite of his dislocated hip he wants more than to have just managed to get away. He wants God to be other than God now is. The demon, the one who suffocates people, the God who exacts satisfaction must be different still. What should "wrestling" with God really mean, other than to press God so hard that God becomes God and lives out more than God's dark side?! Stated simply: Jacob loves God! He wants something from God. He does not leave God as God is. He does not let go. He does not let himself be satisfied with reducing God. He does not say, "That's just the way it is with your God; you can forget him."

> Each of us is blessed
> Let us believe in that
> even if we want to give up
> Give us the brazenness to demand more
> Make us hunger after you
> teach us to pray: I will not leave you
> that simply cannot be everything
> A blessing awaits us.

We ask many times about the meaning of prayer. To wrestle with God in order than God might be God is an answer to this question. To pray means to hold before ourselves again and again the black children of South Africa who today are in prison, humiliated, and tortured. To pray means not to exonerate God. "But, my God, they are your children." Created for freedom, little lower than the angels, daughters and sons of life. You cannot simply let them perish. To make intercession means to remind God of those who have every reason to believe themselves forgotten by God. Wrestling, struggling, praying is a process.

I want to introduce another variation on this theme here. The hymn "Wrestling Jacob" stems from Charles Wesley, the cofounder of the Methodist Church, and relates to our Bible text, yet it turns it around to himself. The "I" of the hymn is alone in his apartment, the guests have left, it is night time. It is a situation we all know. Inside, in internal space, not outside by the river, inside, in the space of the soul:

> Come, O Thou Traveler unknown
> Whom still I hold, but cannot see.

The theme of the attack, of the strange threatening power is transformed here. "With thee all night I mean to stay/And wrestle till the break of day." The second verse then takes up the question game about the name in a manner typical of individualized piety. The question of the angel to Jacob ("What is your name?") is completely omitted; the one praying gives as his name his inner condition: sin and misery, here psychic misery. God knows my name, God has called me by name. God has, as it says in allusion to Isaiah 49:16, written my name on the palms of his hands: "See, I have drawn you on my hands." The one who prays this hymn is so enveloped by God that he does not need, like Jacob, to be asked his name and then renamed. All the weight here falls on the other question which Jacob poses to the nighttime visitor, the man, the demon, the angel, which Charles Wesley poses anew to God: "Who are you?" The praying one, "confident in self-despair," asks God to give his name and thus to bless him. Jacob's two requests for the blessing and for the name are not separated here but blended:

Speak to my heart, in blessing speak;
Be conquered by my instant prayer.
Speak or thou never hence shalt move
And tell me if thy name be Love.

The last verse takes from the Jacob story only the breaking dawn and the fleeing shadow. The dislocated hip is
missing. The name of God, the certainty that God
is named love and is love outshines the darkness. The
unknown wanderer is present. "Pure, universal love
thou art."

Each of us has a secret name
it is written in God's hands
those who love us read it
one day we will be called
land of reconciliation
bank that forgives its debtors
digger of wells in the desert
God's name awaits us.

The story of the fleeing Jacob, who now goes to meet
his deceived brother, out of the drama at Jabbok has
become the meditation of a solitary man. The demon
has become an unknown wanderer or guest, the wrestling match a prayer struggle. The poem is reminiscent
of Rembrandt's conception in his picture "Jakob Wrestling with the Angel." The angel there is a beautiful,
earnest young male figure, who with his large wings is
more protective than threatening. The wrestling match
looks like an embrace: both figures are entwined in one
another, as if Jacob and the angel had become one in
an erotic relationship. This interpretation, in which a
wrestling match is turned into a prayer struggle, is
characteristic of the entire modern era. Prayer is the
place where God is conquered and lets Godself be conquered.

I have difficulties with the expression "struggle with prayer" — it sounds unnatural to me — but it has become progressively clearer to me that praying and struggling do belong together. To wrestle with the dark God for the life of a human being in order that this beloved person may not die, that he no longer turn to the bottle or to the needle, that he not be ruined by self-despair — we are all familiar with this. Is it not true that we pray more when we love more? That we throw ourselves into God's path so that God cannot get away, that we "coerce" God, as the jurists express it, that God might finally be God! "Prove your power, Lord Jesus Christ" (*EKG* 91, 2); do not hide behind proclamations, pronouncements, and promises — these we have known for two thousand years — but speak now and say that your name is love and not terror. Say it in the psychiatric hospital and in Soweto and in Baghdad!

Praying and struggling belong together. Who is the God of Jacob and our God? Who assaults Jacob, and who blesses him? Who comes to us as fate, as disastrous drought, as material constraint, as the stranger, the unknown one who afflicts us? The answer does not lie in theology but rather in the wrestling that we may call prayer or struggle; they amount to the same thing. God assaults us no less than God assaults Jacob. In prayer we present ourselves to the one who assaults us. We are naked; we have sent away that which could protect us. Let yourselves be assaulted by God; do not think that Jabbok lies far away and that other children, not mine, live in Soweto. Everything speaks in favor of struggling with God for God, that God may become visible, that God's sun may rise in us also and we may receive a new name.

NOTE

1. *Evangelisches Kirchengesangbuch,* 140. Hereafter cited in the text as *EKG.*

CHAPTER 5

God's Pain and Ours

AUTHOR ELIE WIESEL has written a drama that traces the "Trial of Shamgorod," as it was held on February 25, 1649.[1] It is the time of the Chmielnicki pogroms in Russia, to which hundreds of thousands of Jews fell victim. In a small village inn near Shamgorod a Purim play is put on according to ancient tradition: three Purim actors present a trial in which God is accused because of the suffering of God's children. The play takes place after a pogrom, but while the players are drinking and, following tradition, celebrating the festival — at which "everything is free" and things may be said which otherwise no one dares to say — bands of murderers are ganging together again outside. Strictly speaking the play takes place in the brief period between two pogroms and treats the theme of theodicy. The three drunken Purim players try in vain to find a defender for God. The prosecutor says: "There is [no defense attorney] — but who is to blame for that? His defenders? He killed them! He massacred His friends and allies! He could have spared Reb Shmuel the dayan, and Reb Yehuda Leib the cantor, and Reb Broukh the teacher, Hersh the sage, and Meilekh the shoemaker! He could have taken care of those who loved Him with all their hearts and believed in Him — in Him alone!

Whose fault is it if the earth has become inhabited by assassins — by assassins alone?"[2]

Toward the end of the play a stranger emerges from the night, an attractive, enigmatic figure named Sam. He is prepared to play God's defender; he affirms God's omnipotence and absoluteness. "I'm His servant. He created the world and me without asking for my opinion; He may do with both whatever He wishes. Our task is to glorify Him, to praise Him, to love Him — in spite of ourselves."[3] While all put on their masks in order finally to begin the play, Sam puts on the mask of the devil, breaks into a long, hearty laugh and gives a sign towards the outside. The door is pushed open and the gang breaks in.

I think this play takes the theme of theodicy more seriously than we who do not know whether we should accuse or defend God. The seriousness is expressed quite falteringly and comically through the allocation of roles: the three drunken Purim players are the judges; the daughter of the innkeeper, who has gone mad as a result of a gang rape, is witness for the prosecution; the old innkeeper, the most devout, is the relentless prosecutor. The accused is absent, "as is his custom," it was once stated ironically. And the clever theologian who defends God turns out to be the devil. He calls himself "God's emissary. I visit creation and bring stories back to Him. I see all things, I watch all men. I cannot do all I want, but I can undo all things."[4]

Prosecution and defense, testimony and judgment represent a mode of thinking in which the leap into the next meta-level is excluded: that is the strength of Wiesel's writing. The question cannot be neutralized or historicized. Must we accuse God? Can we defend God? Is there a defense of God that is not satanic but rather comes out of a great love? Or is the accusation the greatest gesture of love toward God that we can summon up, as it seems in many of Wiesel's figures? Where do we belong in this play?

I pose these questions because I suspect that fixation on the problem of theodicy is an evasion, a denial of suffering. If we remove the problem through a justification of God in the face of the suffering of the innocent, then we deny it in the classic masculine manner of theologians. But there is also a post-Christian philosophic denial which proceeds by historicizing. Then we assign the problem a century in the history of philosophy. The history of the theodicy problem in philosophy is the history of "the progressive distancing or withdrawal of a claim of totality or of a monopoly of interpretation, which corresponds to an increased narrowing of concepts like rationality, discursiveness, and consistency."[5]

Up until well into the modern era the "old European harmony thesis" prevails, "according to which God, but also nature, does not permit pure suffering or evil to exist." The classical answer to the question of suffering is formulated thus by Meister Eckhart: "Everything that the good person suffers for God's sake he suffers in God, and God is with him suffering in his suffering."[6] The unbrokenness expressed here, such an important historical finding by C.-F. Geyer, makes theodicy as yet unnecessary; and where the binding force of religious schemes of interpretation "has been completely dissolved, theodicy is likewise not necessary — any longer — nor is it any longer possible."[7]

God, according to this Eurocentrically understood history, had for a while many defenders, but today prosecution and defense have become unnecessary. In the systems theory of Niklas Luhmann, for example, the meaning of reflection has shrunk to the function of mediating and interpreting the "socially prescribed meaning."[8]

The religious tradition today lives on in the thinkers of critical theory, who negate its content but in "indignation" (Ernst Bloch) or "longing" (Max Horkheimer) have adopted more and more religious substance than their modern atheistic denial of the religious tradition leads us to suspect. Technocratic reason, however, no longer recognizes an identity in the emphatic sense, because it is limited to a "harmony, even if it is only on the surface, of feelings, social groups, economic contrasts." In a certain sense it represents not only the "postmodern" end of the modern philosophy which was still religiously motivated but also the coming to an end of every philosophy which was still related to universal reason. For technocratic-instrumental reason, the question concerning suffering and evil falls "completely out of the realm of philosophy and harks back to those things in which apparently people no longer take comfort."⁹ The practical application of this kind of philosophy today is the so-called "tolerance research," in which it is determined how much pollution and destruction of the living environment the empire can afford in a certain region.

What does this historical review mean for systematic theological thinking?

For a relatively short span of time in the history of Western philosophy, the theodicy thinkers tried to reconcile three qualities of God with one another: omnipotence, love, and comprehensibility. The result of the debate can be summarized by saying that only two of these three theologumena are conceivable, that one must always be excluded.

Either God is omnipotent and comprehensible, insofar as omnipotence can be comprehended by those subject to it. God stands, pictorially speaking, at the head of the universe as the great manager, the one in the know, the one actually responsible; as the one who at

least can step in and end human torment, provided God
wants to. In this context we often speak of the innocent,
of children, for example, who are tormented. But in a
deeper sense all humans are innocent: no one deserves
to starve to death, and not a single one of the six million
who died in the gas chamber — even if they otherwise
lied, stole, or were beasts — ever "deserved" the suffering inflicted on them. An all-powerful God who imposes
suffering, who looks down on Auschwitz from above,
must be a sadist. Such a God stands then on the side
of the victors; and is, in the words of a black theologian
from the U.S., "a white racist."[10] In Wiesel's play that is
the position of Satan: he always emerges where people
are being murdered; he is the advocate of subjection.
His God is sheer power. And a theology which conceives such a supreme governor, organizer, responsible
cause and creator reflects the sadism of those who come
up with it.

The second position conceives of God as indeed
omnipotent and all-loving, but at the same time as
incomprehensible. This God withholds itself from us.
Belief in this God becomes absurd or at best a paradox.
"In the face of Verdun I lost my belief in God," is a
widespread expression of mass atheism as a consequence. If God has become incomprehensible, we cannot
in the long run hold onto such a God anymore, even in
paradoxical faith. This God is dead.

The third position conceives of God as love, but not
as omnipotent. Between the victors and the victims God
is only credible if God stands on the side of the victims
and is thought to be capable of suffering. This position
is represented today by completely different Jewish
thinkers like Elie Wiesel, Abraham Heschel, Hans Jonas,
but also a popular theologian like Rabbi Harold Kushner.[11] On the Christian side I think first of all of Dietrich
Bonhoeffer, who came closer and closer to the suffering

God in prison. I would also mention process theology, which articulates God's neediness and God's becoming, and liberation theology, both in its Latin American as well as its feminist forms.

In what follows I will, in the sense of the third position, direct my thoughts to the suffering God, who alone answers the question about the suffering of the innocent. I want to snatch God out of patriarchy's clinch and overcome the theodicy question as a false question.

My point of departure is the recent and current suffering of people in El Salvador; I observe the hermeneutical principle of liberation theology, namely that the poor are the teachers. From them, not from those who have possessions, make decrees, or hold power, we learn what it means to believe in God. The testimonies of Christians from the Third World play an ever greater role for the universal church (for the ecumenical movement, for instance), but also for theologians of the rich world who long for liberation from their Babylonian captivity. In what direction do these testimonies point with respect to suffering? First I will sketch the suffering of the Salvadorian people.

Of the five million people in El Salvador, one million live as refugees outside the country; a half million have been driven away from their homes in their own country. Most of them belong to the very poor, without education or possibility for work. They possess only what they carry on their own bodies. The military name for this systematic and bloody banishment of the population from their homeland was *Operation Phoenix*. This method was applied earlier in the Vietnam War; it usually begins with the bombing of the civilian population. The army destroys the harvest and people's houses; then the survivors are brought to a camp. "In January 1986," reported one refugee, "they took us captive — and thanks to international pressure and the politics of the new regime people are now no longer murdered but handed over to the Red Cross. So we came here to the camp. But we are not refugees; we do not want to live from charity but to return to the place of our origin. Why does the government want to depopulate the land and lock us up here in the camp?" The answer is clear: only a depopulated country guarantees military victory. The presence of population hinders the counter-insurgency tactics which it has been one of the main goals of the Pentagon in the last twenty-five years to perfect. The bombing attacks on civilians, which rightly or wrongly were suspected of being subsidized, tripled in each of the next two years, that is, under supposed "democracy." The land was made unliveable, harvests burned, civilians killed or forced to flee.

The death squadrons continued to work. No officer who tortures or kills has ever been brought to justice, and Decree No. 50 legalizes torture. Anyone can be taken prisoner by the "security forces," who usually emerge at dawn, mostly in civilian dress, though sometimes in uniform. Those "arrested" without an arrest warrant remain fifteen days in the custody of the secret service and security forces — without a lawyer, without a connection to relatives, for whom they have become one of the "disappeared." After fourteen days at the latest, 100 percent of those arrested sign an extra-juridical confession, in which for example they admit to having possessed automatic weapons or having been a member of the FMLN — a confession which in almost all cases is retracted later before a proper tribunal. What brings these people to make these confessions, which are often furnished with other persons' names and often signed on a blank piece of white paper? The answer is apparent: it is torture, which has gotten its lawful *entrée* through Decree No. 50. Force, terror, torment of people are legalized here. Prisoners are interrogated up to seventy-two hours straight with no food, no water, no sleep, constant light; machine pistols lie next to the questioner; electroshocks are common. Those who are arbitrarily arrested generally have no idea why they were the ones picked out. But it is not up to the state to prove an offence; instead, they must clear themselves of the ever-present suspicion of subversion. As a rule they are also questioned about utterances of priests or other church workers; only the fundamentalist groups of the new religious right are regarded as reliable and loyal to the state. Fear and terror are ever-present.

"Things have changed somewhat," said the pastor of the slum congregation Mary, Mother of the Poor, "but not much. Now they no longer kill bishops, only the leaders of the rural congregations and the catechists. And you can hear the bombs that they drop on the roofs over there. The death squadrons kill fewer now, but the causes of injustice remain the same or have gotten worse. They have become more specialized in torture; there are forty methods of torture. They do it in a more refined manner so that no visible traces remain. Thousands are made refugees, more than ever. For us war brings only annihilation. How is it that for 17,000 persons in this community we don't even have any land?"

What are the theological answers of people to suffering? The vicar general of the San Salvador archdiocese, Monsignor Ricardo Urioste, says to us: "These years of pain have called forth two things: We had the opportunity to see a people who are without any hope within the political situation place their hope in God. And we have understood the church anew and differently. We believe that the poor in El Salvador have seized an option for the church; whether the church has always seized the option for the poor we do not know. In any case it is the poor who evangelize us and preach to us. Often when one feels depressed and just spends a little time with the poor — you cannot imagine how much it changes a person. Three years ago a woman came to me whose daughter and niece had been dragged away. A day later she found both corpses; the heads had been cut off. I didn't know how I should comfort her; my voice failed me, but she began to comfort me. She said to me: 'Monsignor, I simply opened my Bible, I read Psalm 92, and I felt comforted.' I looked up the Psalm when I got home, and for the first time I understood it. God is the only savior. That gives us hope: a people that has faith, not this passive faith, but active. . . . In the church today we need a real conversion."

Perhaps Oscar Romero helped the people in San Salvador most by calling those who had been murdered "martyrs" and thereby giving the people the only illuminating and acceptable interpretation of unimaginable suffering. Padre Daniel works in the parish of Mary, Mother of the Poor; his predecessor was picked up, tortured and finally expelled from the country. Here too fear — even the fear of pronouncing a word like "community" — is present everywhere. "Yesterday we celebrated the annual memorial of the martyrs Padre Octavio Ortiz and Sister Sylvia. That helps us out of the lethargy and deadness that we are in. From suffering comes greater strength. The people here, those who have been resettled and the victims of earthquakes, have developed strong self-confidence. They have the sense of community that we often long for. And how they reach us to serve! Last Saturday I married three couples. They all already have a bunch of children, and I asked them why they wanted to get married. The answer was, 'To serve the community (*al servicio de la communidad*).' It is not only a matter of families. We have founded a housing commission here and build simple huts. When the first houses became ready they were given to widows, not to members of the commission! I can give you hundreds of examples of this sort. Young people fish in the lake, and when they come home they look around for those who cannot go fishing, older women and those with small children, and they bring them fish. I can assure you that in this community there are new social values. People live the gospel, they have hope for the people and trust in the people. They have become the subjects of their history. You can also see it at the festivals they celebrate — in the midst of care and misery they live out joy. God is moving today through Central America. In the hymns of Isaiah the humiliation and scorned one emerges. He was interpreted as the Messiah, as a prophet, or as the people. Even if the people don't know it, they are this suffering servant of God; they are light for us all."

The most important contemporary Salvadorian theologian, Padre Jon Sobrino, also refers to the suffering servant of God. "He had neither form nor beauty that we should look at him" (Isaiah 53:2). The poor have no teeth, they arouse disgust, they do not wash themselves. "He was the most scorned and despised, full of pain and sickness. He was so scorned that people hid their faces from him; therefore we have esteemed him for nothing" (Isaiah 53:3). The servant of God lives among the godless, among corpses. People turn away from him, they reject the victim of torture. The disappeared and the concealed mass graves should remain invisible — Isaiah speaks of that also. "And they gave him his grave with the godless and evildoers, when he died, although there was no deceit in his mouth." "It is for our sins' sake." As the servant of God will be the light for all people, so also the poor further the salvation of others. "The poor," as Jon Sobrino relates, "accept God; they hear the gospel not so much as truth, but as good news. Never have I heard the Mass celebrated so gaily, so jubilantly as in the midst of the poor. They save us, they help us. At the refugee camp *Calle real* they brought in eight large rolls of paper with names written on them. They were the 1064 dead of the community, 80 to 90 percent of them massacred by the army. In the middle they laid a picture of the resurrected Christ. They also had 14 photos of children with them. What they do makes us all more human; it evangelizes us."

"We hear God in the suffering of the poor. That is our 'from below'! But is the First World, structurally speaking, ready for the good news?"

What right have we of the First World, who participate in its indifference and objective cynicism, to ask the theodicy question? To listen to the poor and to learn from them means to change this question. The religious question about suffering is then no longer what we so often hear: How could God permit that? but rather the more difficult question which we have yet to learn: How do our pains become God's pain, and how does God's pain appear in our pains? Insofar as I speak of "God's pain," I free myself from the constrictive thought of patriarchy: God as ruler, God at the peak of hierarchical thinking, God as omnipotence — these theological forms of thinking make me feel disgust and contempt. And the God who is self-sufficient, changeless, eternal, beyond need and vulnerability, can answer the question of human suffering either not at all or only cynically. This God must be indicted, and our longing to defend him runs into a void. Among the intellectual conditions of patriarchy, within the theology of the All-Powerful, the best we can expect is still the dispute over theodicy. Insofar as I try to name God's pain, I put this false thinking right. I am not speaking about something that

God could avoid or do away with. When we speak of God's pain, we employ another concept of God than the purely masculine one. God is then our mother, who cries over what we do to one another and what we do to our brothers and sister, the animals, and plants. God comforts us as a mother does: she cannot charm away our pain (although that also happens occasionally), but she holds us in her lap long enough for us to stand up again and have new energy. God could not comfort us if she were not bound to us in pain, if she did not have this strange and wonderful ability to feel the pain of another on her own body. To suffer with, to be present for another. The gospels describe Jesus as one who has this ability. If someone hits us on the face in his presence, he flinches and feels it on his cheek. If someone is told a lie in his presence, his need for truth is present. If a whole person is suppressed under the brutal power of the empire, he weeps over his city, Jerusalem.

I have just said, with realistic qualifications, "if in his presence." Let us try for once to think about God and take away this limitation. All suffering persons are in the presence of God. There is no "if." God does not forget. The *praesentia dei* is never merely an observing presence but always in pain or joy. Without God's pain, God is not really present but only turns up like the president of a government occasionally visiting the people. But God does participate in our suffering. God is here and suffers with us. Really? In every suffering, every injured vanity, every toothache, every frustration that life inflicts on us. I think that before we can conceive of God's pain and our pain together, we must learn to distinguish them. The New Testament is very clear on this point; Paul distinguishes in Second Corinthians between the "sorrow of the world" and "Godly sorrow" (7:10). Concerning the sorrow of the world, he says that it produces death. It knows no hope, it leads to nothing.

When I think of the sorrow of the world, I think of these terrible illnesses of prosperity, like alcoholism, anorexia, workaholism, to name just a few. These illnesses arise in a climate of prosperity which ignores our non-material needs and manipulates them in such a way that they are transformed into addictive dependencies. People become victims of an apparently rich, well-ordered world and carry its terrible disorder and spiritual impoverishment in their own bodies and souls.

Paul contrasts this "sorrow of the world" with another: "For Godly sorrow produces a repentance that leads to salvation and brings no regret, but worldly sorrow produces death" (2 Cor. 7:10). What is this "affliction as God wills it," this other pain, which not only revolves around itself but calls forth conversion? How are our pains, which so often only express the sorrow of the world, to be distinguished from God's pain?

Is not all pain, every difficult suffering, every kind of torment such a misfortune that we should fight against it as unbearable with all means at our disposal, and if possible remove it or at least make it invisible and suppress it? That is the answer of an atheistic consumer culture. It says: "Away with it! Take the pill! Then get rid of it immediately!" Suffering is pushed away like an annoying shadow. In this scheme of life, the human being is conceived like a machine: it functions, it produces, it runs, or it is broken, doesn't work anymore, and must be replaced either in whole or in part. This technocratic model of machinery dominates our thinking. The machine feels no pain. There are many theologians who seem to me to imagine God like an indestructible supermachine. It supposedly continues to function even after a nuclear war and the destruction of creation. In such fantasies of God I do indeed see the power, greatness, and independence of God expressed nearly perfectly. But I cannot find in this thinking any indication of God's pain or God's connectedness. For this reason I find it difficult, within such thinking, to believe in God's love. The totally transcendent God is not connected to us through pain, and Paul's distinction between the sorrow of the world and godly sorrow (*lypa kata theon*) loses its meaning if no sorrow resides in God.

In the context of Paul's letters, affliction usually refers to the resistance that the apostle as proclaimer of liberation encounters: trickery from the authorities, imprisonment, threats on his life, torture, death. Paul measures the two kinds of sorrow, that of the world and that of God, by what they produce. Godly sorrow arises from the pain of God over a barbaric world filled with injustice and destruction of life. To participate in the pain of God means to perceive God's sorrow. "You have grasped its meaning. What zeal it has awakened in you! You have offered resistance! You were angered and frightened, you have longed for a change, you have forced it to come about and have called the guilty to account" (2 Cor. 7:11).[12] We must read the letters of Paul as documents of resistance against Roman state power, resulting from his belief in the liberating Christ. Signs of the sorrow that God wills, then, are: to be outraged, to offer resistance, to long for change and force it to come about, to call the guilty to account. This sorrow does not revolve around itself and does not brood about itself. It is a sorrow that we find in the hearts of resistance fighters against the destruction of creation and the plundering of the poor. It is the sorrow that was in Martin Luther King, Jr., and in Dag Hammarskjöld, the sense of shock that could not be assuaged over the brutality of a system that wants to function but does not participate in God's pain and does not admit God's vulnerability.

In the Gospel of John also, the presupposed situation

of the Christian community is that of persecution in the Roman Empire. The Christians of this small community at the end of the first century have experienced their life, their everyday existence, as a prison of anxiety. The word "world" no longer carries for them its ancient Greek meaning of cosmos, order, adornment, beauty but rather expresses above all enmity against God, a world full of dangers and lies, a world that hates God, that destroys light and life, that makes the community afraid: "In the world you will have trouble" (John 16:33). Life is without hope, and perhaps Mary Magdalene, in her weeping and continuing to weep, in her inconsolability over the murder of Jesus, is the clearest witness to the pain which determined the Christian minority's feelings about life in this world of persecution and prevailing injustice. Mary Magdalene does not accuse God, she does not defend God; she weeps. That is, she is much deeper in God than an accusation or a defense can be. In order to accuse she would have to be at a distance from God; she would have run away like the male disciples. But she is in God's pain. "Truly, truly, I say to you," says the Johannine Christ, "you will weep and lament, but the world will rejoice" (John 16:20). Those who rejoice are those who greet the triumphal parades of the Roman emperors joyfully when a small nation is again forced to its knees, ravaged, violated, and sold into slavery. The world will rejoice — those are the splendid gladiator fights and sports shows that the Romans hold in order to divert attention from the misery of hunger. "You will weep and lament," because in a world of legitimized force every word that speaks seriously of righteousness and peace is dashed and derided. The Romans knew precisely what a threat the Christian congregations represented for the religio-political state consensus.

The visit that I made to El Salvador helped me understand the New Testament better. In this tiny land under the military heel of the Imperium, the poor weep and mourn when their crops are burned and when their teachers and union organizers are dragged away and made to disappear. And when the secret service and the security forces can torture prisoners at will and without interference for two weeks under Decree No. 50. "You will weep, but the world will rejoice." At the same time, television, firmly in the hand of the Imperium and its local collaborators, carries sports and style shows. Every day $1.5 million flowed into the tiny country mainly as military aid, supposedly for pacification yet in reality for the war against the people. A million and a half daily for napalm and electric torture devices, for low-flying airplanes that force the population to flee, for watchtowers and barbed wire, for military boots and blood.

God's pain and our pains — in El Salvador the pains of the poor are also the pains of God. God suffers with them and transforms their pain. God will free them, God will heal the land. The most important image which the Bible uses for God's pain in the world is an image from the experience of women, an image of giving birth. In the context of the prophecy of the servant of God in Second Isaiah, we read: "For a long time I have held my peace, I have kept still and restrained myself, now I will cry out like a woman in travail. . . . And I will lead the blind in a way that they know not, in paths that they have not known I will guide them. I will turn the darkness before them into light, the rough places into level ground. These are the things I will do, and I will not forsake them" (Isaiah 42:14, 16 RSV).

"You will be sorrowful," we read in John 16, "but your sorrow will turn into joy. When a woman is in travail she has sorrow, because her hour has come; but when she is delivered of the child, she no longer remembers the anguish, for joy that a child is born into the world. So you have sorrow now, but I will see you again and your hearts will rejoice, and no one will take your joy from you" (20b–22, RSV).

How does this transformation from fruitless, meaningless pain to God's pain occur? How do people move from stomach pains to labor pains that usher in a birth? How does our pain connect with God's pain? And how does God's pain light up our pain?

Once I walked late in the evening along an isolated street in Manhattan. A beggar was squatting on a bundle of rags, and I was afraid of this old black man. When I gave him something, he raised his head, looked at me and said clearly and with great dignity, "God bless you." I was moved, but I did not know why. Today I would like to say that God's pain was visible in his pain. By taking part, my pain became another pain. My fear left me. My anger returned. Everything that Paul says to the Corinthians about the sorrow that comes from God was present; I was indignant and shocked by this everyday street scene. "You have offered resistance, you have longed for a chance and have called the guilty to account . . ." (2 Cor. 7:11). I knew again why I would like to convert the people that I meet to peace and why I no longer want to endure the hatred and deterrent terrorism of those who in our day tremble on account of their image of the enemy. The old man, who has no shelter in the richest country on earth and in history, evangelizes me. He elicits my pain for his country, which I love and respect. But I also mourn for my country, which has betrayed its soul in greed for more weapons, in the neurotic search for more security. My disgust at the world in which I live, at its brutality and greed for more death, engulfs me. And in the midst of this world of ever more elegant and more widely disseminated advertisements for the beauty of fighter bombers and tanks; in the midst of this world, under an industry (the profits of the industry of death) of unlimited economic growth, which learned nothing from Chernobyl; in the midst of this gleaming and perfect lie, I am no longer alone with my sorrow. God's pain encircles my pain, and the sorrow in which we live today becomes a strength which binds us in solidarity for the struggle. My strength grows out of my grief. My entire effort is directed toward transforming the "sorrow of the world." It would be asking too much to think we could reorganize the grief which reaches into the depths. It would also be asking too little, because the "sorrow of the world" would then be dissolved only by the joys of this world, essentially the joys of having, possessing, using, and consuming.

I believe it is our task to change the "sorrow of the world" into God's pain, and with God's pain I notice a strange experience. Even though the pain is not tempered, soothed, or denied, it still brings me to a deep joy. It is as if I were touching with my own hands the power of life as it also lies within pain, which is the biological protest of life against sickness and death and which hurts us so on account of life. I am not speaking about a robotic God who will send joy again after pain and sun after rain: I see the sun within the rain. I do not wish to go in search of strength outside of pain; that would be to separate myself from God and to betray God's pain. "The people who walk in darkness see a great light, and those who dwell in a land of deep darkness, on them the light shines" (Isaiah 9:2). Where does such a statement come from, if not from God's pain! How can we see darkness and light together, if not in the one who embraces both!

Someone might object: "I hear the music of which you are speaking, but why should I connect the pain which it expresses with what you call God? I have no use for this concept." To this friend I would like to say: "If the pain were only pain, I could not label it God's pain. But because it is oriented toward joy, because it is borne up by joy, I therefore call it God's pain." This meeting of opposites, joy and pain, this *coincidentia oppositorum* is very difficult to express in our language, because we use another logic for it than the usual logic. The experience of such a pain is in fact close to the overwhelming inner experience of birth. To bring a child "into the world," to give birth, is an original experience in which we come very close to the mystery of life. It is an experience that we undergo and carry out; we participate passively and actively. It is an experience which challenges body, spirit, and soul and can change one deeply. It is one of the great experiences of creation in which we participate. It is a mystical experience, because in the face of it we are standing before the mystery of life itself. This mystery of life is what religions call "God," and my religious tradition includes pain in the mystery of life. It places pain within God's heart. It is the "participation in the powerlessness of God in the world" to which Jesus calls — that is the legacy of the martyr and theologian Dietrich Bonhoeffer.[13]

If we want to move from the sorrow of the world to the sorrow of God, we must learn to perceive God's pain. Then our question will also run: How do I act toward the nameless suffering which I cause? What position do I take toward the dealings which my bank carries out with torturers and racists? How do I deal with the large-scale destruction of foodstuffs? Where am I implicated in the war industry (which Bertha von Suttner straightforwardly calls the "death industry")? How much energy do I use and at whose expense? How long can I bear to be an accomplice in an unjust system?

All these questions belong to the question of suffering. We cannot afford to stick these questions into a political box and our personal questions about suffering into another box, as if we only had to deal with God within the scope of the private box. If we think thus, then we take away from God the possibility of drawing our pain into God's pain; then we make ourselves incapable of participating in God's pain and experiencing it as labor pains.

We do not want to remove the sorrow of this world and our pains with the methods of this world, with sedatives. For in the middle of our pain, God calls us to God's kingdom. God will bind up our personal story into God's own great good story. How can that happen?

Pater Alfredo is a priest in a base community in Guatemala. In lifting two full water cannisters, his back could not stand the weight, and in carrying them he popped a vertebra. A terrible pain overcame him, and painkilling means were not available for miles around. The priest lay for five days and five nights on his bed, crippled by pain. He told his friends that he wanted to offer this suffering "in sacrifice" to Christ. A sick woman who has great pains is asked by her spiritual advisor not to curse her suffering but to bear it in patience, because then the fruit of her suffering increases the treasure of the church.

Earlier, in my enlightened Protestantism, I used to smile at this custom and the theology that lies behind it. Later I criticized its awful abuse, by which the poor and especially women are supposed to be held in eternal submissiveness. Today, as I try to overcome the bourgeois-individualistic understanding of suffering, I am much closer to this thought. I understand Alfredo better. It is not technology, he seems to say to me, which makes life bearable, but rather a changed attitude toward suffering. It is not technological hope — in the right medication, a good doctor, the newest method — which helps us, as good as it is and as much as Padre Alfredo himself fights for it in his revolutionary work. But really to handle suffering, we need theological hope, which ties our pain to God's pain.

In many traditions of human history, voluntary suffering has been thought to have a purifying, reconciling, salvific power. The nonviolent movement of Mahatma Gandhi and of Martin Luther King, Jr., always believed in the power of such suffering. Our small beginning in the West German peace movement — among those who blockade, let themselves be arrested and sentenced to a fine or imprisonment — feeds on this belief in the power and persuasive strength of suffering undergone voluntarily.

This basic thought is alive in the Catholic devotional practice of sacrificial suffering, and indeed it is extended in that now the suffering which was inflicted or forced on us can be changed by us and made into voluntary suffering. We add it to the church's treasure store of grace which was provided by Christ. Two elements in this practical theology of suffering are illuminating to me — the elements of freedom and of solidarity. Suffering is not only endured, it is appropriated. Thus it becomes a part of my life, a part of my freedom. I am free to go around grim, frustrated, despairing with my suffering or to "offer it up to Christ." The priest Pater Alfredo chose to live for the poor and with the poor who have no painkilling medicines. By understanding the accidental brutal suffering on his bed of pain now in the light of Christ, by giving it to Christ, he makes it into an element of his freedom. He also does not live simply as a casualty, a torment to himself and a burden for others. Rather, even now he lives God's special preference for the poor. His personal pain becomes a part of God's pain.

The second theological element that becomes visible here is community. Suffering is deprivatized. It does not belong only to a broken-down body. It becomes a part of everyone's life. By giving it to God, it works to the benefit of all. You suffer not only for yourself alone, not only for the educational purpose of your own self-improvement, as it is often thought in Protestantism.

"And whom should that benefit?" we may still ask in our rationalistic obsession with results. I believe it benefits Alfredo, because it allows him not to write off these days and nights of his pain as meaningless, unproductive losses. It benefits him in living now as a human being, not as a cast-off. "If my suffering is in God, and if God suffers with me, how then can my suffering be misfortune?" asks Meister Eckhart.[14] It also benefits those who see and hear Pater Alfredo. Perhaps they will become different, more awake, and they will pray for and work toward getting a health station in the region. And it benefits God when something is presented to God. Pater Alfredo thereby helps God to carry God's pain. He shares God's pain.

NOTES

1. This text appeared in Marco Olivetti, ed., *Teodicea Oggi?* Archivo de Filosofia LVI:1–3 (Rome: Cedam, 1988).

2. Elie Wiesel, *The Trial of God*, trans. by Marion Wiesel (New York: Schocken Books, 1979), 103–104.

3. Ibid., 157.

4. Ibid., 158.

5. C.-F. Geyer, *Leid und Böses in philosophischen Deutungen* (Munich, 1983), p. 196.

6. Meister Eckhart, *Deutsche Predigten und Traktate*, ed. J. Quint, 3rd ed. (Munich, 1969), 133.

7. Geyer, 107.

8. Ibid., 172.

9. Ibid., 194.
10. William R. Jones, *Is God a White Racist? A Preamble to Black Theology* (New York: Doubleday, 1973).
11. Harold Kushner, *When Bad Things Happen to Good People* (New York, 1982).
12. I am indebted to Jorg Zink in my reading of this passage.
13. Dietrich Bonhoeffer, *Letters and Papers from Prison*, ed. by Eberhard Bethge (New York: Macmillan, 1971), 362 (letter of July 18, 1944).
14. Meister Eckhart, 133.

Chapter 6

Christ, the Man for Others

THE SPIRIT of our time raises many questions of the
Christian faith. Some are posed with words, in conversations and discussions. But more frequently they are
posed, so to speak, with feet in either secret or open
withdrawal from the church. It is these latter questions
that concern me here. Though most are not articulated,
they are quite critical questions in a deeper sense.

When I try to explain to non-church-going people
why I am "still," as they usually say, a Christian, I begin
to reflect back over three phases of my own religious
development which seem to me to be typical of the
behavior of people in industrial culture.

Most of us go through the first phase during childhood if we are brought up according to the religious
norms and customs as well as the beliefs and practices
of our ancestors. The religious sensibility of our ancestors arose in the cultural climate of the small town or
village, where the church stood at the center of social
and intellectual life. Myths and legends, values and ethi-
cal norms, were rooted and centered in traditions which
were simply accepted. I call this religious phase that of
the village. Even today there are still people who spend
their whole religious life "in the village." But the great
majority emigrate to the big city, if not in reality then

at least from the standpoint of feeling: they have ceased to pray and to go to church.

In this second phase, religion slowly but surely loses its power over people. It either falls into oblivion or becomes the focus of a conscious critique in which people ask themselves how they can be freed from a religion which was thrust upon them or how they can be healed from "God poisoning" (Tilmann Moser). In this second phase most throw off their religious heritage and live as post-Christian citizens in a secular city.

The history of religion, however, does not end with this departure, this urbanization, this industrialization. The contradictions of life in the city, the rootlessness, the disintegration of rituals and customs which are necessary for life make many people insecure and send them on a search for *religio* (binding back), for undamaged roots. Where should they turn? Back to the village perhaps, as churches often recommend? Back to the worn-out authorities and rules? To the pipe organs and confirmation rites? I think that there is yet a third phase. After the religious security in the village, after the religion-free departure into the cold city, people decide consciously for new forms of religion. Today they are still in the minority, but the number of those who are devout — albeit not in the sense of the old village — will grow. Two things seem to me important for this third phase of religious consciousness. First, it is a *conscious* religious decision. The religion of the village was inherited; one was born into it. But the new forms of religion — whether they be Christian or Eastern or from some other cultural horizon — are consciously chosen. That religion today can no longer be inherited is a result of the Enlightenment and of this human migration into the city.

A second element is closely connected with this: the decision in favour of a religious conviction happens critically, not naively. We do not accept everything; we act selectively, making choices. Gottfried von Lessing already understood this when he asked: "Should I then swallow the carton with the medicine?" Must I believe and follow each word in the Bible? The answer to this is a clear no. Even the strictest Bible believers do not marry the wife of their brother when he dies! With the departure from the religious village, authority — of the pastor, scripture, or the official church — is gone; it cannot be reinstituted. Anyone who comes to a critical affirmation of faith after an intensive debate in the second phase is now also struggling for the development of new forms of religious life.

I suspect that many today are on the way from phase two to phase three. Within the Christian women's movement and feminist theology, above all, there is a search which cannot be dismissed as authoritarian, as back to the village, to paternal or clerical authority. But also outside of the Western Christian horizon, many people are involved in a search for a new religious house, for new forms and rituals, for spirituality in a completely different language, for new models and new forms of expression. I know a number of young people whose parents still had to struggle with the transition from phase one to phase two and who then at first were relieved to settle into the largely religion-free big city. Their sons and daughters no longer have anything to do with these clashes; they tell me enthusiastically about Zen meditation, about a Sufi master, and so forth. They look for gurus, teachers, masters, models. Often they identify Christianity so much with the village of their grandparents that they consider it to be beyond hope. I then try to tell them and the other inhabitants of the secular and boring city something about Jesus — the rigidified cliché, yet completely unknown master, guru, teacher, model, liberator of the Christian tradition. I try to make them appreciate devotion to Jesus and also the teachings about Jesus.

The technical term for reflection about Jesus Christ is christology, and so I have chosen three common questions which I have experienced as personal probings. By proceeding through them I want to try to present a christology which, I am convinced, can emerge today only in dialogue with Christians of other regions of the world, that is, ecumenically. Because I believe I have learned something from these Christians of the poor world, it will have to be a christology "from below."

Many years ago, when I was still a small shy student, I asked a man at a construction site, "Do you happen to know what time it is?" He gave me such a strange answer that at that time I was completely speechless. "Am I Jesus?" he said in a kind of good-humored mockery. Always when I reflect on who this Jesus, let alone this Christ is supposed to be for us today, this man with his question gets in my way. Am I Jesus?!

For this worker, Jesus is from another world. A heavenly being who has nothing to do with us, who sees, hears, knows and can do everything. The churchly language, which has called him Messiah, Lord, Son of God, the Christ, gets its due here. That's what you get, I would like to say to the thinkers and fathers of the faith, when you make Jesus into an unreachable, completely other Superman, indeed into God! That is precisely what comes out below from your steep christology which celebrates the Godness of Jesus at the expense of his humanness so that nothing reasonable is left over, at most a Sunday outing of the heavenly being who stopped by for a short visit in Bethlehem. Christology from above, which stars with the Godly side of Jesus and makes of him an all-knowing immortal, ends in "docetism," as that false teaching is called in technical

theological language, which recognizes Jesus' humanness and above all his suffering as appearance only.

This false manner of deifying Jesus is quite common
among us. As a young teacher of religion I once asked
the schoolchildren whether they thought the baby Jesus
also had wet diapers. Most children rejected that decis-
ively. Jesus, already even as the Christ child, must be
different, higher, purer. My own children believed for a
long time that the Christ child was a girl. This kind of
children's religion is indeed gratifying in the feeling that
Jesus incorporates both the masculine and the feminine.
But it also suggests the image of an unreal, genderless
being — as if Jesus were something other than a true,
ordinary person like all of us. Martin Luther insisted on
drawing Christ "into the flesh," and it was for just that
reason that I spoke of wet diapers! But high christology
draws Jesus away from this world; he becomes unreachable, incomparable. And above all we cannot live as he
lived — we shouldn't even try, because it's impossible
anyway. How would we ever manage to feed the
hungry? When we ourselves don't have much more
than five loaves and two fishes? How would we ever
manage not to serve the industry of death? Or how
would we manage to heal the lepers? Are we Jesus?!

Today I would answer the worker at the construction
site a little more openly and take the initiative. "Naturally," I would say, "you are Jesus, man! What else
would you want to make of your life?! Being yourself
alone isn't sufficient — you know that already! You too
are born and have come into the world to witness to
the truth. Don't make yourself smaller than you are. We
have enough fellow-travelers already. Just imagine: you
and I and your mother-in-law and your boss — are
Jesus. What would change? There's something in us . . .
of God."

That is how I would talk today and in so doing think

about what the Quakers with their strange expression call "that of God in you." Because in actuality we cannot understand Christ if we do not believe and accept "that of God" in each person. "If Christ is born a thousand times in Bethlehem/And not in you/You remain still eternally lost," writes Angelus Silesius. To the question "Am I Jesus?" the answer can only be: "Yes, why shouldn't I be?"

I want to mention a second kind of modern inquiry into the role of Jesus. Once when I was preparing for Christmas, an American non-Christian woman asked me: "What is so special about Christmas? That a man comes into the world and regards himself as God — what's new about that?" In this remark there are two important critiques of the Christianity that has been handed down. One is a critique of patriarchy, the other of its hero worship. The main lie of patriarchy consists in confusing man with human being. Many have still not yet understood that the likeness of God in the Bible was not a man, Adam, but two human beings, Adam and Eve. According to this religion, therefore, God's characteristics must be just as feminine as masculine. Would Jesus have come to divert us from this truth? Would he want to give his blessing to the adulation of men and sanctify three male symbols in the name of "Father, Son and Spirit"?

Yet even this critique of the theology and doctrine of Jesus thinks "from above." The real Jesus in the Gospels did not regard himself as God unless perhaps in the sense of the mystics, to which I just alluded. Jesus was a devout Jew who lived and spoke out of the power of God. He did not use his consciousness of God to hold himself up as something better, to let himself be served, to shove himself into the foreground. He was not equipped with miraculous powers that always func-tioned; in Nazareth, where no one believed in him, he was not able to heal. It was no easier for him to believe in God than it is for us. He did not inherit any psychological lead.

But within the critique of the man who comes into the world and regards himself as God there lies still another question which can be called that regarding christolatry, or idolizing of Christ. Why do we need heroes, gurus, wise men, or leaders anyhow? How is someone who lived two thousand years ago supposed to be the decisive occurrence for everyone, those who live later and, in many speculations about Christ, also those who lived earlier? Do we really need a savior, a king, a conqueror, a redeemer? Someone who does everything that we cannot, who loves when we can no longer love, hopes when we give up, lives when we die? This question is difficult to answer, and I believe in fact that we need more for living than just ourselves. The individualism which lies behind the question must be criticized. But again the tradition of a christology from above is more of an impediment. We do not need another conqueror, judge, or hero. Nor is a redeemer needed if the word means that some overpowering person transplants me out of the miserable position in which I find myself into a good, unscathed other world without my cooperation. These caricatures of being saved through Christ surely cannot be what is intended!

To redeem in the Bible amounts to the same as to liberate or save or heal. Christ is not the superhero who suddenly and magically makes cancer or nuclear weapons go away. But he does free us from the fear of being possessed by evil, and he heals by taking away our anxiety, which blocks our healing power. To redeem means to set free the power of God, "that of God" in us; therefore the redeemed are those who insist on their human dignity. "When I get to heaven," sang the black slaves in the South, "then I'm going to run around freely everywhere; no one will throw me out." The liberating Christ of these people kept their human dignity, their hunger and thirst for righteousness alive.

The goal of the Christian religion is not the idolizing of Christ, not christolatry, but that we all "are in Christ," as the mystical expression goes, that we have a part in the life of Christ. This savior is a wounded healer, and he heals so that we may become as he is. Be as he is, laugh as he laughs, weep as he weeps. Heal the sick, even those who without knowing it have contracted the great neuroses of our society, who knows no mercy with themselves and their children when they consent to the nuclear state and technologies inimical to life. To feed the hungry means to do away with militarism. To bless the children means to leave the trees standing for them.

Christolatry is the opposite of what it means to be "in Christ." Søren Kierkegaard practiced this distinction between those who esteem Christ and those who follow him. If I esteem him then I lift him ever higher and have nothing to do with him; I use my admiration to keep myself free of Christ. He is big, I am dependent on him, yet I do not want to go his way. But if I try to follow him, then he never calls to me saying, "Leave well enough alone; you can't do anything anyway. I have already settled everything once for all time." His language is completely different from that of the dogmaticians: "Come along," he says, and that above all. "Come along into God's kingdom — to our home country, where no one is beaten, no one is thrown out and shoved away. Look and see," he says to me and shows how the lame begin to walk. He does not say, "Close your eyes; I'll do everything."

My relationship to Christ is thus not that of a personality cult à la Joseph Stalin or Adolf Hitler. I am with him on the way, but here I must more correctly say "we," because that corresponds to my experience of resistance and working for God's kingdom. We who get involved in him and regard his as the right way are with him on the way. We do not marvel; we go with him. He is our "first-born brother," as Paul says. Latin American devotion expresses this nicely: less is being said today about Christ the King (*Cristo rey*), and more about *compañero cristo*.

In a certain sense the word "Christ" thus expresses a collective meaning. If Jesus of Nazareth was the poor man from Galilee who was tortured to death, then Christ is that which cannot be destroyed, which came into the world with him and lives through us in him. When I say Christ, I always think also of Francis of Assisi and Hildegard of Bingen and Martin Luther King, Jr., and of Ita Ford, the American nun who was murdered in El Salvador — as well as of all resistance fighters who are sitting in prison today. Christ is a name which for me expresses solidarity, hence suffering with, struggling with. Christ is the mysterious power which was in Jesus and which continues on and sometimes makes us into "fools in Christ," who, without hope of success and without an objective, share life with others. Share bread, shelter, anxiety, and joy. Jesus' attitude toward life was that it cannot be possessed, hoarded, safeguarded. What we can do with life is to share it, pass it along, get it as a gift and give it on.

With this I am at a third inquiry from outside regarding the enthusiasm for Jesus which lives in the church as correctly understood. Once in a theological-political discussion I referred to Jesus, at which point an older man who had been silent up to this point entered in: "What do you want with this Jesus? He didn't accomplish anything! I have nothing at all against him, but he didn't succeed. He was killed, like many others before and after him. I don't understand why you want to follow him. Do you want to be on the cross, too?" This man was a skeptical, non-believing Jew. I tried to say: "The killing didn't completely work, as you see. He still lives here and now, too." But it was one of the conversations in which skepticism and faith, tangled up together, wrestle with each other without result.

Naturally my conversation partner was correct in his historically based skepticism. Not only was Jesus condemned and murdered at that time, but Christ still dies over and over again before our eyes. He has been buried in our churches, corrupted to the point of being unrecognizable within the political parties that decorate themselves with his name, and distorted in the symbols, like the sign of the cross, that have been used to murder the innocent. Yet I want to hold on to this Jesus in and with the community of believers. And actually I would like to win for him the three persons about whom I have written: the worker who says, "Am I Jesus?," the woman who despairs of the male management in the male church, and the Jewish skeptic for whom the course of history refutes Jesus and shows his plan a failure. Not because I consider the questions of these contemporaries wrong — I am just as distrustful of docetism and christolatry as they — but rather because this Jesus has a secret which makes him strong and has given me strength again and again. In what does this secret consist? Why can he not be killed either by his enemies or even by his friends?

Christian tradition has tried to formulate this mystery with the words "the Anointed of the Lord," "Messiah," "Son of God," "God the Son"; and it has named Christ in a paradox "true man" and "true God" at the same time. But when we proceed from "true God," there is danger that we will lose the "true man." If, on the other hand, we think "from below," completely different things than "Messiah," "Lord," "Savior," and "Redeemer" become important. Then it is possible to see who this Jesus really was: the illegitimate son of a poor girl, a teenager; a worker who belonged to the landless; a poor man in every sense of the word, living among poor, insignificant people, a nobody from a provincial town; a crackpot who was "out of his mind," as his family decided; a subversive who was sought by the authorities; a political prisoner who was tortured and finally condemned to death. The picture which arises in this way from the actual social history of the gospels does not resemble the victor or judge who is crowned with signs of imperial power. It is more like the emaciated peasant of the great German Peasants' War, as Matthias Grünewald depicted Jesus. The mystery of Christ is the mystery of the suffering, the impoverished, the landless of the Third World, whom we in the rich lands sell into debtors' slavery for generations. Without this affiliation with the poor, without having taken up the fate of the poor to be arrested arbitrarily, interrogated meticulously, tortured and killed — as happens to the *campesinos* in Latin America, the textile workers in Taiwan or South Korea, the black children in Soweto and many other places — one cannot understand Jesus. One cannot hear the call, "Come follow me!" if one's ears are closed to the cry of the poor and their demands for justice.

In what does the mystery of Jesus consist? How can we name that which could and cannot be destroyed? I think that different times have necessarily coined different formulas in order to discover this contagious power in the midst of defeats and in despair. A christological formula that helps me was advanced by Dietrich Bonhoeffer. Bonhoeffer called Christ a "man for others." This is not meant as false selflessness, such as is often demanded of and forced upon women. This man-for-others could indeed say "I" in a tremendously provocative way, putting his "But I say to you ..." against a tradition, pronouncing his "I am ... the water of life, the light of the world." He meant God's water, he meant God's light. He let this light shine through himself, he did not hide it in the depths of his soul, he gave it out. He was the man-for-others because he was the man of God and knew himself to be so borne up by God that he did not fall out of God, not even when he felt himself abandoned by God. The old formula "true man" is rendered by Bonhoeffer as "man," whereas being "true God" is called by Bonhoeffer simply being there "for others," because God is for others the God of love. Thus the sentence, "Christ is the man for others," is the old christological formula "true God and true man" in contemporary speech which refers to God without using religious formulas. The man for others is the man after God's heart.

In the dark night of the cross, life, God's Spirit, of which we are also capable, was with him — in spite of his lack of success. There is a point in Christian understanding when the question of success has to take a back seat to that of truth. Thus I can — with the old skeptic — doubt the success of Christ, but not his truth, which invites me to join him at his side. Thus we do not love this poor Jesus of Nazareth because he was victorious or left the world behind, but rather because his manner of being there as the man-for-others touches us to the bottom of our heart. Indeed that is the intent with us, too. "Love him who burns with love," one hymn reads. Every other reason, for example that he was God's Son, did many miracles, rose and will in the end be victorious, is too weak. The mystery of Jesus cannot be derived from God, but vice versa: his call, his "Come follow me!" or "Pick up your bed and walk!" draws us into God. Christ lets us see into God's heart.

To believe the truth of the man-for-others and thus to take his God is the way of christology from below.

Chapter 7

Cross and Resurrection

THE CHRISTIAN GOD is no little Chinese god of fortune, in whose kingdom it is possible to remain free of want and suffering. If Jesus had just kept to multiplying loaves of bread and healing the sick, perhaps we could have had this illusion. Instead he identified with the suffering and came down with their diseases. For the sake of the suffering he was wronged; in order to overcome death he entered into death. To venture onto the path of Jesus involves finding another relationship to suffering.

In the 1960s British psychiatrist Ronald Laing described the relationship of humans to suffering in a short poem:

> Take this pill
> it takes away the pain
> it takes away the life
> you're better off without

Today I hear many say:

> Take the soft deity
> it needs no cross no blood
> it sweeps you away smiling
> into the land without fear

I want to describe three religious positions with regard

to suffering. The first is the sado-masochistic theo-ideology of God as a hangman; the second is the painfree dream of the soft deity; the third is the faith and hope that binds people to the poor man from Nazareth.

It is not difficult to establish sadistic traits in the picture of God the Lord as it has been passed down. A kind of metaphysics of the death penalty is celebrated there, and the God who decrees suffering is praised. It has to be God himself there who crucifies poor Jesus or "hands him over." God can only forgive there when blood has flowed. In such theology the cross expresses above all the relationship between the Father and the Son; the fact that it was an instrument of the power of Imperial Rome is deemed incidental. Male theologians have let themselves get carried away with comparisons between the sacrificial offering of Isaac, which was demanded of Abraham but then in the end commuted, and the sacrificial offering of Jesus, which the supreme hangman in no way gave back. Their God carried out the blood sacrifice consistently, going to the extreme, even with harsh consequences for himself.

There is in fact a "God who stands on blood." That is why film director Martin Scorsese needed so much ketchup for his film. His cinematic *Last Temptation of Christ* questions profoundly and renews highmindedly the most miserable theology — and it is no accident that the film is extremely anti-women. "There is only one woman in the world, with a thousand faces..." For that reason the Jesus of the film does not need to mourn when the first object drops out through death. I could consider that pathological misogyny, but it has roots in the male projection of God and its false understanding of the cross. Greek novelist Nikos Kazantzakis assures us that we stand "in an eternal battle between spirit and flesh." From this — unbiblical — basis it becomes clear who must take over the role of *spirit* and who the role of *flesh*. Sexism seeks out its justification in a barbaric theology from above.

But is this miserable result of male theology still operative? Living in an enlightened northern metropolis, I can no longer regard *this* danger as so threatening. Suffering is no longer projected onto an Almighty Power who decrees it but rather is understood as the expression of insufficiency — whether it be of antidepressants or of condoms. An actual confrontation with suffering does not take place. The "soft God" appeared long ago, positive thinking has been announced, and the old glorification of suffering no longer holds.

Our culture invites us not to see the cross. We should live in apartheid, take pleasure in beautiful beaches, styles, and recipes — that is what I deduce from the magazines directed at women. The cross is then played down as a purely religious symbol in the ecclesiastical realm: it rests peacefully in gold on the breast of a bishop, and even if someday it should rest peacefully between the breasts of a female bishop, not much will have been won.

But the cross is not "something religious" — it is a terrible, bloody reality. It stands with the small girl who was sexually abused by her father and lives many years in the silence of denial. The cross means the merciless violence which people carry out on people, the strong on the weak, rich on the poor, agile on the clumsy, men on women, women on children, caretakers on the sick, the powerful on the powerless. It is the violence with which the military takes away our recreational areas and trains our sons to kill. It surrounds us, penetrates our lives. And if we deny it, then we begin not really to see ourselves correctly. We deny something in ourselves; and that which has been denied, forgotten, and suppressed grows and chokes us.

Naturally we can continue to live even in this choked

condition, but we would then have destroyed something which our tradition has called the "tree of life." And who would really want to breathe without the tree of life? In the words of an old hymn,

> Tree of beauty, most beautiful tree,
> Your shame is past,
> Your purple branches
> Now call forth life.

How has that happened? How can the tree of life grow out of suffering, out of caprice, out of violence endured? How does the instrument of torture used by the Roman military administration become a tree of life?

The cross expresses the bitter, realistic depth of faith and is a symbol of this-worldliness and history. It was not theologians who invented the cross; rather, the Roman Empire thought up this method of deterring people who heard the cry for liberation by slowly and publicly torturing to death those who cried out. Anyone who has ever read reports of torture, for example from Guatemala, anyone who has seen a film like "Two Worlds" about South Africa knows that it is not a matter of something exotic but of the normality of imperial suppression which now presents a slow method of torture as "low intensity conflict" for whole regions.

It was not God who erected the cross but the lords of this world, whether they are named Pharaoh or Somoza, Pilate or Botha. To go in search of a soft God seems to me like an attempt to emigrate to a distant South Sea island, as if there were no nuclear weapons tests there and no grooming of women for the prostitution trade. The soft God has long been here; I cannot imagine him any softer than our brother from Nazareth. But the actual problem that we have with Jesus and the cross is our wish to get *away*, to hide with the Father.

It is not God who makes us suffer. But love has its

price. God wants to make us alive, and the wider we open our hearts to others or the more audibly we cry out against the injustice which rules over us, the more difficult our life in the rich society of injustice becomes. Even a small love of a few trees, of seals, or of school-children who cry out at night in torment from low-flying aircraft is costly. Many cannot afford even a small love for creatures and prefer not to have seen anything.

And yet there is still today this opposite experience of many Christian men and women: these persons treat themselves to kindness and permit themselves the bit of justice and care for others without which we cannot become human.

There are among us people who allow themselves the truth. They step in for the victims of violence; they create unrest while the authorities are trying to keep everything nicely under control. There is great inner freedom in choosing life even when this choice plunges us into difficulties, unpleasantness, indeed suffering.

I would like to say something in praise of this freedom because I believe that we misunderstand the cross when we make it into a necrophilic, death-seeking symbol. We not only get ill at the cross, we are free to avoid the cross in the apartheid of the middle class or to take it upon ourselves with all the difficulties we enter into when we get seriously involved.

Jesus too was free to go as far as the cross: he could have remained peacefully in Galilee; his friends urged him to avoid the cross. Women whom I know in Nicaragua could have gone to Miami or let themselves be recruited by the C.I.A. No one forced them to remain with the revolution. Members of their families, mostly men, did in fact take the road to the golf courses of Miami. But the women stayed and tried to do the will of God; this original act of freedom has its price. For them the cross is a symbol of the love of life in justice.

It expresses love for the endangered, threatened life of God in our world.

The more you grow into love, into the message of Jesus — to say it in such traditional, defenseless terms — the more vulnerable you make yourself. You simply become more open to attack when you have become conspicuous or when "that of God" lights up in you. When you spread your life around rather than hoarding it, then the great light becomes visible within you. To be sure, you enter into loneliness, often you lose friends, a standard of living, a job, or a secure career, but at the same time you are changed. And the cross, this sign of isolation, of shame, of abandonment becomes, in this process, the tree of life, which you no longer like to be without at all. The dead wood of martyrdom begins to turn green. And you know at once where you belong.

To choose life means to embrace the cross. It means to put up with the cross, the difficulties, the lack of success, the fear of standing alone. Tradition has never promised us a rose garden. To embrace the cross today means to grow into resistance. And the cross will turn green and blossom. We survive the cross. We grow in suffering. We *are* the tree of life.

This understanding of the cross leads us also into a deep comprehension of what for many is often strange talk about the Resurrection. There is hardly any other article of belief with which people today have greater problems than with the Resurrection. When a young journalist once called me up and wanted to know whether Jesus really had risen from the dead, I was puzzled by this very old question. He explained it to me: theologians mostly talk around it, but he couldn't go to his editor with that! Now did Jesus really rise on Easter, or is the whole thing just a fairy tale? What would change for you, I asked in return, if the answer were yes or no? Great astonishment on his part: That would certainly put the foundation of belief into question. I stuck with my question: Assume Jesus did not come forth from the grave — after all, there are no valid proofs for it. Witnesses who saw him, male and female, were all, as we know, believers, partisans, sympathizers, thus by no means objective observers. What does that change for those who believe in him? Or for those who go with him, who feel themselves supported by his truth? I think nothing at all changes, came the answer.

Assuming Jesus was only apparently dead and was revived, would that change my relation to this Jesus? Assuming further that everything in the Bible is literally true, would there then be more Christians? Would Christians be more credible then, and would they look a little more redeemed? I think not. I found the question, which was posed after a scholarly discussion that has lasted for over two hundred years, to be somewhat off the mark. One result of this discussion is the unprovable character of the Resurrection. Supposing photography had existed then, the film would have been blank. I gave the journalist two reasons why I had no desire to discuss the Resurrection on this level.

The first reason is the cross, which may not be separated from the Resurrection if one wants to keep to the meaning of the matter. Belief in the Resurrection roots us in ancient history and in our own history. Easter does not celebrate a departure into a post-history which has finally been attained, something following historical suffering. It celebrates history itself, this emergence from not being free. Without the early history recounted in the Hebrew Bible, the departure of the children of Israel from the house of slavery in Egypt, one cannot understand the departure of Jesus from the house of the dead.

The other reason is my own life, which I do not want to separate from the death and life of Jesus, nor from the defeat and victory of the life of God. Easter is either

105

existential, or else it says nothing at all and is rightfully commercialized.

Whether apparent death, resuscitation, and breaking through the laws of nature are a secure foundation for that which occurred two thousand years ago in Palestine, I do not know. But I am completely certain that this kind of discussion is a clever diversion from something else, namely from the judicial murder of the poor wretch from Nazareth. What we know objectively is that he — like many before and after him — was tortured to death slowly and extremely cruelly. He could, as I said, have avoided this through flight, withdrawal into privacy, transcendental meditation, or other modes of escaping reality. Instead he stuck with the cause, faithful to the love of those whose rights and possessions had been taken, the "last," as he liked to call them. For these last, for those who were regarded as the dregs, he, with female and male friends, developed a new manner of living. He did not want to have it better than the poorest. Therefore he lived without violence and without protection from violence.

Then as today that was not allowed. The consequences from the Imperium toward this attempt at another life were brutal, just like today. Archbishop Oscar Romero, a friend of Jesus, was also "crucified," murdered by the helpers of the state power as he celebrated Mass. The approximately 30,000 people who annually celebrate the day of his death call again and again: "Oscar Romero lives! He is with us. He is resurrected in his people. He stands by us." Is that a fairy tale which the people cling to only because they are poor and ignorant? Or is that the truth of their lives, for which they are prepared to live, fight, and even die? In the prayers and songs, in the marches and protests from the distant land whose coffee we drink, the Resurrection becomes visible.

The Resurrection cannot be discussed in isolation, as if it had nothing to do with the cross. As If Jesus would in any case, even if he had died of old age, have gotten the benefit of this wonder drug. If we keep before our eyes what this puzzling phrase "resurrected from the dead" says, then the reality "cross" belongs to it: whoever lives in love has to reckon with contempt, abuse, discrimination, even with death. In this other way of living, the Resurrection is already visible long before death. Jesus believed above all — and for all — in a life *before* death. The Resurrection, this spark of life, was already in him. And only because of this God-in-him were they unable to kill him. It simply did not function. Even today the powerful do not succeed in extinguishing this love of justice, this sustained interest in the "last."

If we ask ourselves whether Jesus as a clinically dead person was resuscitated, that is a speculation for our scientific curiosity. It does not affect us at all. False thinking — whether fairy tales or facts — occupy us completely from outside and keep us from ourselves. More correctly stated, the question reads: "Is Jesus dead or is he still alive? Does he still bring something about? Does he change people's lives? Can one still say, 'Jesus lives, and in him I live also'?"

Only those who themselves have been resurrected can actually celebrate Easter. Goethe said this in Faust's Easter walk: "They celebrate the Resurrection/For they themselves today are risen." And then Faust details where and from what oppression and truncation of life the people come: "From airless rooms in huddled houses / From drudgery at counters and benches / From under cumbrous roofs and gables / From crowded, suffocating alleys / From the mouldering dimness of the churches / All are brought forth into brightness."[1]

Are there still today experiences of liberation that are more than individual? That would be a serious question after the festival of the Resurrection. Experiences like those from El Salvador and other countries of the oppressed world occur to me. What about in my own country, Germany? I shall again go to the Easter march which still at least identifies the cross, from the terrorism of low-level flights to grandiose transactions with exported weapons. The number of those who in this way experience a piece of resurrection from present-day death is becoming negligible. But on that first Easter morning, too, not many were present.

NOTE

1. Johann Wolfgang von Goethe, *Faust: A Tragedy, Part One*, trans. by Martin Greenberg (New Haven: Yale University Press, 1992), 29–30.

CHAPTER 8

Loving God

IN RECENT centuries religion has been thoroughly and relevantly criticized within the Western world. The three great "masters of suspicion," as Paul Ricoeur calls them — Karl Marx, Sigmund Freud, and Fredrich Nietzsche — have exposed religion as the opiate of the people, as collective neurosis, and as Platonism for the people. Theology — and here I am speaking of its enlightened, Protestant form — has integrated this critique more and more. It has "stepped through the stream of fire"[1] and in its own turn developed a hermeneutic of suspicion, learning self- and institutional criticism, thus always debating anew a critical understanding of Bible and church. Living Christian faith lost its naiveté and its missionary imperialism in this process, and it learned to apply the prophetic critique of cultic worship and sacrificial offerings, of the "noise of your songs," as the prophet Amos expressed it (Amos 5:23) to Christianity and to the church, which must always be in the process of reforming. *Ecclesia semper reformanda!*

This critical consciousness of Christian women and men today, in a paradigm shift which moves from liberal to liberation theology, is increasingly coming up against the real forces and powers of destruction, which have long since ceased to be religion and the church. Money and power need religious legitimation less and less today; it is in the name of progress and technical rationality that they function best. In this situation one must ask whether the traditional critique of religion has not in many respects run its course, because it disregards and does not at all scrutinize the actual religion in which the overwhelming majority of people in industrialized countries believe. This actual religion is science. It has its larger temples, as everyone who has at any time set foot in Harvard University, with its white columns and imposing halls, its main and side altars, its sacred relics and treasuries can tell. It has its own priests, high priests, and popes. It carries out certain rituals, honours and humiliations, which run according to prescribed patterns. And it pronounces what is sinful and what is holy. There is only one thing about which it has learned very little: the critique of its own religion. The question of who benefits from certain research plans is generally rejected as unscientific; analysis of priorities and of the practical application of research, above all for militarism, is considered irrelevant.

If science is now the chief religion of the industrialized world, then I must confess myself to be a nonbeliever. It has not prevented wars but has instead improved the capacity for killing. It has not fed the starving but has instead turned toward space. It has generated a megamachine which rapes all of nature, everything created. It believes in its own second creation, which is supposed to be better than the first. The visions of science have long since turned to horror stories; I call to mind only the current scientific approach to torture as a method of investigation. Is it sufficient in this age to think scientifically? Do we not need another approach to the world, other placement of the values which scientists put into service? Indeed, isn't theology, which in the words of Walter Benjamin has

110

today become small and ugly, needed more than ever in order to gain some other vision of the good life as a way of living together without domination?

Religion and wholeness stand in immediate connection, which is always painfully clear to me when someone wants to insinuate to me that religion is my "very personal hobby" or believes it necessary to deal with my "special religious interests." I feel then that this wholeness is trivialized and compartmentalized, as if religion were a kind of elective subject next to economics, sexuality, environment, and politics, and not a universal human behavior.

If this were so and religion were an elective subject, which many quite early opt out of, then it would contribute more to the deepening of division than to wholeness. But to me it seems precisely the opposite: religious language is not something highly specialized like the third Minoan culture but rather the best expression of my wish to be whole, to live with my whole heart. It is precisely not to hold my own as a specialist in economics, sexuality, work, and culture but to make my contribution as a living, feeling human being, who strives first for the kingdom of God and God's righteousness. Religion does not pull me out of the whole but rather lets me be on the lookout directly for it and to miss it when it is absent.

In this context I will try to say what I believe in.

In liberation theology we often speak of "God's preference for the poor," the *opción preferential por los pobres.* Perhaps there are in all religions such "options," chosen decisions of an obligatory character, and I understand the Christian faith, which I confess, as an *opción preferential por la vida,* a preference for life over against death. Being is better than nonbeing, kissing is better than nonkissing, eating is not only preferable to going hungry but ontologically superior. This ontological surplus of Being in the face of Nothingness is what the Christian religion also tries to articulate.

As I was trying to explain this kind of belief in life to a friend inclined to depression, he shook his head wearily. "You only want to entice me again toward creation with almond blossoms and moonrises." In fact that was and is my intention. The ontological priority of Being over Nothingness is expressed religiously as faith in the creator God and in the good and blessed creation. God saw on the sixth day that everything "was very good." God's option proceeds from life; it is with these eyes of God that I too want to see, without denying — still, as I then add in faith — that which fatally contradicts this vision. No accident brought us onto this small blue planet; life itself calls to us to participate in life in a thankfulness which does not cease even in darkness to perceive life as a gift, as grace. To praise life is a kind of devotion toward existence which I need and which I try to convey.

I believe in God, in the creative energy that "calls into existence the things that do not exist" (Romans 4:17), that is good and wants the good for us, which means being whole and flourishing in our ability to reflect God. The German word *glauben* (to believe) comes from the word *geloben* (to vow) and does not have as its first meaning the rational connotation of "to accept, to hold as true," but rather an existential dimension of "to promise oneself to someone." I believe in God for God's good creation, as it was intended, with equality of man and woman, with responsibility for tending and preserving the garden, with our ability to work and to love and thus to be the image of God.

The origin is at the same time the goal. Since we come from God, we also enter into God. Each day we take steps toward this reality of God. We recover partisanship for life from the triviality of the everyday and the trivialization of our life's goals and wishes. This recovery is what my tradition calls *teshuva*, or conversion, and one of the deepest experiences and hopes of the faith is the assumption — not guaranteed by anything secular — that we are capable of conversion. I should believe that of myself; disbelief in the possibility of one's own conversion is perhaps the worst thing that depression does to my friend. I am summoned and invited to think my neighbor capable of this conversion, even if he or she stubbornly continues on a course headed straight for an iceberg; and I should even think the enemies of life capable of this *teshuva*, which in fact is an absurd undertaking in view of the obsession with which the rulers of this world pursue the project of death. Yet I do believe the tradition it posits conversion as our true possibility.

How, though, am I supposed to love God, praise and preserve creation, and take an active part in the kingdom without despairing? The help which my tradition offers to me is called Christ. I find it relatively easy to believe in him. One doesn't need to be a Christian in the fundamentalist sense of the word in order to be drawn to his path, and one doesn't have to make the dogmatic distortions of his truth into a central issue. He himself never considered the exclusivity of his own person to be the issue but rather what he saw beginning to appear: God's kingdom. We are all sons and daughters of God; he is only the "first-born among many brothers and sisters" (Romans 8:29), who opened up the God of Israel to the Gentiles of the ancient world. His bonds to the foundation of all life were strong enough and are present in everything that we know of him; his orientation toward the goal is unambiguous. In his short public life he became more and more the love of which he spoke. To believe in Christ does not mean to marvel at him as a hero but to follow him. "Let this mind be in you which was also in Christ Jesus" (Philippians 2:5 KJV).

But did he not fail completely? Was he not, along with his dream of God, betrayed and denied, condemned and tortured to death? And has not his project of the kingdom, in the church which followed from it, been more than ever betrayed and denied, defaced and burned a thousandfold? As if the ancient Christians had suspected what would become of the church and in what despair this apparatus would have to plunge the female disciples of the poor man from Nazareth, they added to the ground of life, and to the leader and finisher of life, still another puzzling figure of the faith, the Spirit of God. We say better today, following the Hebrew meaning of the word, the female Spirit, *ruach*, which makes alive.

I cannot imagine my life without belief in the *ruach*. Reason, if it doesn't conduct itself merely as a neutral observer, runs aground in despair. If it is honest, it can only run aground, given the death project which now as before dominates science, the most important productive force. From what should the minorities of conscience, who combat the suction of death, who intercede for trees and butterflies and water for their grandchildren, who let themselves be arrested and sentenced in nonviolent resistance, derive real hope? I think it is not overstated to see the *ruach*, the Spirit of God, in the resistance against everything that wants to reconcile us with death. According to tradition, the Holy Spirit gives two things: truth and courage. Truth means that God's Spirit intends human beings to be capable of truth. It is not as if we could not know, as if the experts were eternal rulers and judges over a people regarded from a faithless perspective as dumb and unsuspecting. When in the beginning of the 1980s natural scientists and doctors constituted themselves "for peace," I had to smile a bit. My experience was that housewives in church congregations had grasped much earlier that starving children cannot be kept alive with bombs and poison gas. The *ruach* had made them capable of truth, and that says a great deal in a world of systematic, state-decreed *disinformation*, as a new term for lies goes. God's Spirit, by giving human beings truth and freeing them from the deep fear of being incapable of truth, also led them on to courage.

I often find the present to be wrapped up by a blanket by the mild depression of intelligent people, in which they are incapable of action because they remain without faith. The supposed material constraints of the industrialized world, and the corresponding experiences of impotence in people who know "one can't do anything," exacerbate each other. Knowledge has degenerated more and more into knowledge of death. Even enlightenment alone does not suffice because it cannot overcome the dominant spiritlessness. To believe in God's Spirit means above all to call, "Come, Holy Spirit . . . ," even in our emptiness and in our dependence on the drugs with which we have surrounded ourselves. Another life *is* possible; the heart of stone *can* become a heart of flesh. To believe in this possibility is indispensable for my life. I become engaged to the Spirit precisely when in my own present within the bounds of my class, my people, my role in world history, I feel a little of her fire.

I want here to draw upon an original testimony for this trans-subjective experience, in which the need for foundation, for a wholeness filled with Spirit was expressed. It is in the *Sh'ma Israel*, the confession of the one and only God, which every devout Jew prays daily:

Hear, O Israel!
The Lord is our God, the Lord alone.
You shall love the Lord your God
with all your heart and with all your soul
and with all your might.
Take to heart these instructions
with which I charge you this day.
Impress them upon your children.
Recite them when you stay at home
and when you are away,
when you lie down and when you get up.
Bind them as a sign on your hand
and let them serve as a symbol on your forehead;
inscribe them on the doorposts of your house and on
your gates. (Deut 6:4–9[2])

What does it mean to love God "with the whole
heart, the whole soul, the whole spirit and with all your
strength"? It is the basis of what many today like to call
holism, undividedness, oneness, connectedness with the
whole. If one has a deep need to find the verbs,
the action words, which finally give hands and feet
to the ideals denoted by such great nouns as freedom,
equality, and brotherliness or sisterliness, then I would
like to say that the verb for the vision of "wholeness"
is: to love God above all things. In love of God we
move forward out of the division, the alienation, the
indifference, the spiritual apartheid toward wholeness,
which in religious language is called salvation.

The Protestant tradition has become too colorless to
be very helpful, because it scarcely dares to articulate
love *toward* God and only speaks of the love which we
receive *from* God. The fact that only those who can give
themselves can "receive" in the deep sense of the word
goes unnoticed by rigid orthodoxy. But it is in the un-
divided love toward God that the holistic connection to

life grows. Love for God is the wish to give oneself fully to the meaning of life and to carry out this great surrender to God's life in the world without curtailing, denying, or repudiating some strengths that are also within us. Wholeness is another word for devotion. To be devout means to give oneself to God, to take part in the movement of love in the world and to become love oneself.

This wholeness of our surrender is impossible as long as we have to struggle with our unconscious feelings and not allow ourselves to recognize and change them. To be whole would mean to be present with our feelings and with our knowledge of this world. But how is that possible? We live in a system of undernourishment and overkill, to put it concisely. We profit from this. The huge animal from the abyss reigns over us.

The true love of God must place itself within the reality in which we live. It is not possible for it to look aside joyfully and self-assuredly from the reality of hunger, for example. The natural reaction to self-made chaos is fear and the desire to suppress. The reality of dying forests, perishing seals, and at the same time the military air shows which are still celebrated make it difficult for us to live holistically. They force us into repression. I no longer want to know how much pesticide is in my blueberries and which disease we could heal for the cost of another fighter plane. How much energy I have to put into denial and repression!

In this sense I am no better than my fathers and mothers in Nazi Germany who also "didn't know anything." I am shocked, I want to forget, I have to repress, I have my feelings of anxiety to repress and to push aside as quickly as possible. I call this condition fear of fear. It cripples me and makes me into a powerless being — a person who cannot give herself to the mighty stream of love and into the struggle. The fear of fear finishes me off: between me and love is fear and the fear of fear. In 1 John 4:18 I read: "There is no fear in love, but perfect love costs out fear." But that is not true for me: my love is too weak to drive out fear, and instead fear dominates me as the strongest impediment to loving God "with all my soul."

I don't want to have any idea what happens with my water, or with my grandchildren. Where would I be if I had to know all that! And thus, in the middle class of the rich world, this conflict of cultural appeasement in the interest of spiritual apartheid — the hypocrisy that we encounter at almost every party — grows precisely out of the desire to be whole in an intact world.

But the desire to be at least somewhat whole, to act with all our strength, cannot be stamped out or manipulated away. There are signs of a new search for another, integrated form of life which does not constantly proceed at the cost of other living beings or elements.

The desire to live with our whole heart, to love God with all our strength even between 9:00 and 5:00, to be in accordance with God also on Tuesdays in the production and management of the life that we are pursuing, to live, think, feel and act holistically, moves toward a new devotion to life which is in harmony with nature. It can be felt at many points.

One of the basic principles of classical aesthetics says that only what proceeds from our gathered strengths can be called "beautiful." "Everything which is isolated is reprehensible," as Goethe says. Every separation of a single human potentiality, every overdevelopment of one strength at the cost of others is "isolation." The isolation of rationality requires that we suppress or deny our corporeality and our emotionality. Every expression of life, for example every human relationship as well as every creative activity, should be "whole" — that is, it should engage all our strengths. The more of myself

that I forget, deny, repress and suppress in one relationship, the more partial, the more limited, the more impoverished will be the relationship. One-dimensionality
is the expression of such prevailing impoverishment and
destruction. Although it can attain a specific perfection,
it lacks the beauty which stems from the ensemble of
our strengths, experiences, and relationships. A human
being becomes beautiful in the experience of the wholeness of his or her strengths, in uninhibited teamwork.

One of the principles of New Age spirituality is formulated by Gunther Schiwy as follows: "Since in nature
everything is connected with everything, and the past
as well as the future is enfolded within God's present,
you will expand your limited ego-consciousness to an
unlimited self-awareness, and from this you will act
with self-awareness."[3] The point of departure for holism
is nature, in which everything is connected with everything: the amount of energy that I waste, or that I allow
those who occupy our air space to waste, changes the
past (for example, of the species which are condemned
to extinction), and dictates the conditions of the
future — as if the earth belonged to us like a shoe
factory belongs to the factory owner. If, on the other
hand, we understand ourselves to be focal points of
divine-human consciousness in the universe, possessing
and using things at our disposal ceases to be essential
conduct toward the world. Holism is a deep connectedness with everything that lives. The new consciousness
of "dynamic holism" experiences the implicit, enfolded
order and lives according to it.

Here I want to name three characteristics of the new
devotion and to try to say in what sense those who
uphold them live differently, more holistically:

■ The unimportance of material values, an indifference — astonishing for the generation of scarcity —

toward material incentives and rewards, a new form of incorruptibility, and an often vague search for spirituality.

■ Skepticism toward science and technology, which are understood as means for subjugating nature and controlling people. The productive side of this skepticism is not demonization of technology but affirmation of "soft" technologies.

■ An orientation toward nature which is different in principle, the readiness to protect it, even to enter into a covenant with it against the powers inimical to life.

The questions which are raised concerning this new devotion from the perspective of the Jewish and Christian traditions do not criticize the new relationship to nature nor the pantheistic element, without which a serious correction of nature imperialism is unthinkable. What is to be questioned instead is from the prophetic tradition of the Bible: the lack of an element of justice. The holistic devotion of the New Age does not articulate that every yoke will be broken. It takes its wholeness from nature and not from the humbled and offended "neighbor," made in the image of God. It does criticize modern individualism, just as it criticizes the atomistic worldview of the old science. But lacking in its holism are the elements of struggle and suffering; they often seem like the pain-free enthusiasts whom Paul criticized in his Second Letter to the Corinthians. Where the spirit of God is, so they seem to say, there is harmony, wholeness, fulfillment, light within us. There hunger and those who cause it play no role; there the highest value appears to be self-actualization. For Paul this is a false path which takes a short-cut from Christ to God and avoids the cross. As if the Imperium with its obsession with armament and pauperization would tomorrow collapse completely by itself! Within the biblical tradition, in any case, "loving God with one's whole heart" was accomplished differently, with the justice which in fact requires all our thoughts and wishes, our rationality and our emotions, our fantasy and our perseverence.

NOTES

1. [Translator's note: This is a play on the name of Ludwig Feuerbach, another nineteenth-century critic of religion.]
2. *Tanakh: The Holy Scriptures. The New JPS Translation according to the Traditional Hebrew Text* (Philadelphia: Jewish Publication Society, 1988).
3. Internationale Pedagogische Werktagung, Salzburg, 1988).

CHAPTER 9

Trusting God

A FEW years ago a friend sent me a welcome greeting when I arrived in New York City: "Welcome to Babylon on the Hudson." We still live in Babylon. We live in a rich and cultured city, surrounded by the newest technologies and luxury goods, far away from the city of Jerusalem, far away from everything that we could perhaps call "homeland."

Second Isaiah, the prophet who lived around 550 years before Christ, belonged to a part of the Jewish people that was carried off from the homeland in Jerusalem to exile in Babylon. "By the waters of Babylon we sat down and wept," sang the displaced Jews, full of homesickness for Jerusalem.

This exile is understood by Second Isaiah as a punishment from God: the Jews lived in servanthood and had to do slave labor. They were a small people under the rule of great powers, without self-determination, without sovereignty. It is into this situation that Isaiah speaks of the return from exile. "Comfort, comfort my people! says your God. Speak tenderly to Jerusalem, and cry to her that her time of bondage is over, that her penalty is paid; she has received at the Lord's hand double for all her sins" (Isaiah 40:1–2).

God wants to comfort the people. The time of punishment is supposed to come to an end. The exiled are supposed to be allowed to return home. In spite of the guilt and in spite of all transitoriness, of which the prophet knows, God speaks comfort to the people. God speaks to the whole people, not just some few who find themselves in a particularly bad situation, but the nation in subjection, the nation under a military superpower, the nation without hope.

We too live in Babylon. The people of God in Germany, Holland, and Switzerland live in Babylon. When will we come home out of this Babylon bristling with weapons and out of this industrialism into the land that we used to call home, in which one could eat apples from the trees and swim in the rivers? We too live in Babylon. I do not speak of the majority of the populace, which still backs progress and power and has adapted to the Babylonian lifestyle. I speak of the people of God as I experience it: a minority of people, steadily increasing, who live their lives as exiles in this our land with ever clearer knowledge of the death that governs us: we cannot have both children and bombs, both assurance of basic needs for all and the gigantic profit of the Babylonians. I am speaking of the too soft, frequently too plaintive resistance against the murder of our earthly homeland, of our brothers and sisters the animals and plants. I am speaking of the Christians in our country with whom I am associated, the people at Church Congresses (*Kirchentage*) and in small parish circles, the people at Greenpeace and Amnesty International, the hundreds of thousands of young people who do not want to bring any more children into the world and who have the apocalypse in full view, who are treated with tear gas if they resist, or who hand themselves over to alcohol and drugs if in desperation they close their eyes. I am speaking of the people of God in Western Europe, of our fear and our impotence.

I believe that knowledge of death among the populace has multiplied tenfold in recent years; it can simply no longer be overlooked. What, though, are we doing with our knowledge of death, with our experience of impotence, with our cowardice? We sit there like paralyzed rabbits facing the snake. This paralysis, this fear, this consciousness of impotence is the spiritual problem of our time. We simply do not believe Christ, who said to the despairing disciples: "Everything is possible to those who believe." Can we then believe the prophet Isaiah, who says to the people weeping at the rivers of Babylon, "Comfort, comfort my people"? "Have courage, it cannot go on like this." Isaiah hears a voice in the desert. This voice recalls the foundational experience of the Jewish people, who had already once experienced emigration, becoming free from foreign rule and coercion; they had already once gotten free from the authority of a military superpower. The people of God have their memory of the Exodus, the departure from the house of slavery in Egypt. And this greatest memory — that God makes people free — is connected with the greatest vision of the people of Israel, the vision of the coming of the Messiah. "Comfort my people," says God, and with the comfort comes the call, the vocation. With the gift comes the task.

Comfort and justice are not split apart in the Bible such that the church should ease difficult fate for individual persons with the newest psychotherapeutic methods and leave justice to the leading industrial nations. God does not come with cheap consolation, like a comforting lollipop from heaven. God does not console in such a way that we get something shoved into our mouths to quiet us down. What, then, is comfort really? When my children were still small, I once wanted to console my third daughter with a chocolate rabbit. At which she said to me, "Mama, you just want to pacify me!" I have never forgotten that, I was so appalled at myself.

God does not want to pacify us but to encourage us so that we may share in God's power. Isaiah says: "For the glory of the Lord shall be revealed, and all flesh will see it together, for the mouth of the Lord has spoken it."

The glory of God, the splendor, the fullness of God—I prefer to translate this mysterious word with "the beauty of God." To be comforted does not mean that we receive something, a thing, an object from God but that we catch sight of the beauty and splendor of God. Where, then, do we see that? Where can we find that?

The Bible is quite clear on this point. The beauty, the splendor of God is visible in all those who prepare God's way. The messianic work of liberation awaits us. God entrusts us with preparing the way of the Messiah. God does not say to anyone, "You are just a simple housewife or a mere employee and understand nothing of complicated necessities." Prepare the way of God, comfort the people in their weakness, make them into street workers on God's way. No man is too small or too large, no woman is too young or too old, too educated or too ignorant. God has given all of us a part, God comforts us, and we prepare God's way. God's voice calls to us and we answer. God's spirit wants to make us courageous and capable of truth. God wants to be born in us.

CPSIA information can be obtained
at www.ICGtesting.com
Printed in the USA
BVHW030611260322
632262BV00010B/257